basis

506(c) - Proof offered
$500

REAL ESTATE
TAX DEFERRAL
STRATEGIES
UTILIZING THE DELAWARE STATUTORY TRUST (DST)

PAUL M. GETTY

ISBN: 978-1-48359-187-2 (Print)

ISBN: 978-1-48359-188-9 (ebook)

CONTENTS

Tax Deferral Strategies Utilizing the Delaware Statutory Trust

"For those new to DST's and DST investing, Paul Getty has provided an easy to digest, practical guide that covers the waterfront of this type of investing. An excellent first step in becoming an accomplished DST investor!"

"Paul has done an excellent job in 'demystifying' an aspect of real estate investment that should be considered by anyone looking to derive income from real estate."

— Rob R. Kaplan, Jr., attorney and co-founder of Kaplan Voekler Cunningham & Frank PLC

"In this readable book, Paul Getty describes the current use of a Delaware Statutory Trusts, or DST, to defer taxes in exchanges under Section 1031 of the Internal Revenue Code. As described in the book, the DST has become the structure of choice for exchangers, having surpassed the older, more cumbersome Tenant in Common, or TIC, structure. The book summarizes the background and substance of past and present exchange programs, with numerous illustrations. By reading this book, exchangers and their advisors will jumpstart their education into the pre-ferred replacement property structure for the last remaining method of deferring gain on sale of investment property."

— Louis Rogers, CEO and Founder, Capital Square 1031, LLC

"In this comprehensive book, Paul Getty has provided a user-friendly guide to help investors understand the IRC Section 1031 tax deferred exchange rules and time requirements along with an in-depth analysis of Delaware Statutory Trusts (DST) which has become an increasing pop-ular and sought after replacement property alternative. Paul's book, in addition to having many excellent illustrations and examples, provides a thorough resource for real estate investors desiring tax deferral and the benefits of passive ownership in the DST structure. Readers will glean valuable insights from Paul's many years of expertise and will be armed with excellent questions to ask financial advisors as they evaluate various

DST offerings. This is a top-notch resource that I highly recommend for real estate investors!"

— Scott Saunders, Senior Vice President - Asset Preservation, Inc.

"DSTs are an important tool for investors to know about, whether for converting to passive investing or as fallbacks approaching exchange deadlines."

— Ron Ricard, Vice President Investment Property Exchange Services, Inc. (IPX1031®)

"Leveraging years of real estate investment and management experience, Paul Getty offers sage guidance to accredited investors looking to optimize their ownership of real estate. Here is the power of 1031 Exchanges described in plain language."

— Brandon L. Raatikka, JD, Vice President FactRight, LLC

Paul's latest book is an excellent introduction into tax deferral strategies and Delaware Statutory Trusts and would benefit both the seasoned investor as well as those seeking passive investment strategies. The book is an easy read with insightful tips and useful information for both investors and advisors desiring to better evaluate investment options. Congratulations to Getty for bringing together an informative, must read, book for those wanting to learn more about the complexities of Delaware Statutory Trust investments. - Well Done!

— David M. Fogg, Esquire, Eagle Law Center, LLC

FOREWORD

Investment strategies utilizing the 1031 Exchange are used by many investors to achieve their investment goals. Income-producing real estate in a Delaware Statutory Trust (DST) structure has become a desirable alternative for accredited investors seeking income and asset preservation without the headaches that can accompany wholly owned investment properties. Use of a 1031 Exchange further improves potential returns on the sale of income-producing real estate by allowing a deferral of capital gains taxes, which effectively allows investors to reinvest a larger portion of their gains, thereby improving the growth of their net worth.

The rapid growth of this form of investment in recent years has created a need for increased education on the part of financial advisors, investors, lawyers, accountants, and other intermediaries to better determine the suitability of this option as part of an overall investment strategy.

Paul Getty has done an excellent job of clearly discussing the pros and cons of the DST structure as well as laying out a sensible roadmap for finding and evaluating DST options. The book also contains useful background on the 1031 Exchange process, including examples of common transactions that can yield a deferral of taxes and thereby further enhance investor returns. Even those investors who have completed previous 1031 Exchanges can benefit from taking time to read and study the advice and best practices contained in this book.

As a national broker-dealer firm operating in all fifty states, we are interacting with a growing number of investors seeking higher-income options than may be available through more traditional investments in equities and bonds. Rental income derived from real estate investments has the possible added benefit of depreciation and expense write-offs that can produce higher after-tax income than other forms of investment.

The Delaware Statutory Trust structure has emerged as a very popular option to obtain higher net monthly income plus grow net worth using a 1031 Exchange upon sale of the underlying assets.

I highly recommend this book as a means of learning more about how DSTs may be an attractive investment option.

Chet Hebert
Chairman and CEO
Colorado Financial Services Corporation
December 2016

ABOUT THE AUTHOR

Paul M. Getty is a co-founder of First Guardian Group (FGG) in 2003 (www.FirstGuardianGroup.com), a national real estate investment and management firm that has completed more than $1 billion in trans-actions. FGG's business lines include commercial development, 1031 Exchange, management, leasing, financing, and sales brokerage. He has been an active venture capitalist with technology investment firms Venture Navigation and Satwik Ventures. His prior operating experi-ence spans over twenty-five years as a serial entrepreneur and execu-tive officer in firms that resulted in investor returns of more than $700 million through multiple successful initial public offerings and mergers and acquisitions.

Paul is a frequent speaker on investment topics at industry conferences. He is the author of *The 12 Magic Slides* (Apress, 2013) and a co-au-thor of *Regulation A+: How the JOBs Act Creates Opportunities for Entrepreneurs and Investors* (Apress, 2015).

Paul is a licensed real estate broker and holds Series 22, 62, and 63 securities licenses. He has an MBA in finance from the University of Michigan, with honors, and a bachelor's degree in chemistry from Wayne State University.

ACKNOWLEDGMENTS

I would like to acknowledge the help of all the people involved in this project who provided comments, critiques, corrections, and other useful input. Without their support, the overall content would have lacked many important perspectives that I believe make the book more readable and understandable to all types of readers.

I would like to first thank my wife and long-time business partner, Jan Getty, for her ongoing efforts in keeping the project on track and ensuring that I succeeded in producing a highly useful book that would meet the needs of a diverse group of readers. I would also like thank members of my office staff at First Guardian Group, who committed significant time and support over the long process of researching and completing the book, including Dinesh Gupta, Jason Hogin, Laura Ede, and Erik Carlson.

Lastly, I would to acknowledge the valuable input from the publisher, who aided in finalizing the formatting, cover design, and layout of the book.

CHAPTER

1

INTRODUCTION

Real estate investments in income-producing properties remain one of the most solid and reliable sources of building net worth. Investors have discovered that income from real estate benefits from tax advantages that are not available to other classes of investments, such as stocks and bonds. Not only can somewhat higher gross returns be achieved, ranging from 5% to 7%, but other key benefits can be realized as well, including:

- Income can be protected from taxes through depreciation and expense right-offs.
- Taxes on appreciated gains can be deferred and potentially avoided altogether through a 1031 Exchange.
- Overall returns can be turbocharged using leverage (debt).
- Day-to-day volatility is lower and less affected by market corrections.
- Real estate is a tangible asset with inherent scarcity and uniqueness.

Even in dark periods such as the global financial crisis in 2008, where virtually all asset values plummeted, income from real estate investments remained positive due to tenant occupancy, which remained favorable.

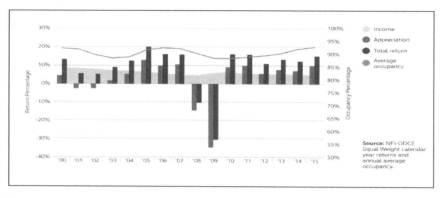

Figure 1.1

The NCREIF Index, which measures the performance of U.S. commercial real estate properties, reported an annual return of 12.7% in 2015, which outpaced other key indexes such as the S&P 500, the Dow 30, and the Russell 2000. Over the past fifteen years, including the 2008 meltdown, the NCREIF Index reported an average annual return of 8.8%, which is 200 basis points higher than the S&P 500 during the same period.[1]

One of the first principles learned by all investors is the inherent trade-off between return and risk, i.e., the greater the return, the greater the risk—and the inverse: the lower the risk, the lower the return. With experience, however, many investors learn and apply techniques that can increase their returns without necessarily raising their risk of loss. One of the most common ways of achieving higher returns without added risk is to take advantage of existing tax laws that favor the treatment of certain types of investments over others, thereby allowing investors to keep a higher percentage of their gains.

While the U.S. tax code contains thousands of such preferential tax advantages for many types of investments, ranging from making movies

---

1The National Council of Real Estate Investment Fiduciaries (NCREIF) is a member-driven, not-for-profit association that improves private real estate investment industry knowledge by providing transparent and consistent data, performance measurement, analytics, standards and education. See http:// www.ncreif.org/ for further information.

to investing in municipal debt, one of the largest remaining areas of favorable tax treatment is real estate.

The range and degree of tax advantages has declined from the high tax years of the 1980s, when real estate investments were often done even if the investment did not make a return because allowed write-offs could be taken for several times the amount of the original investment. While tax reforms have since eliminated these extreme advantages, today's real estate investors are still allowed to significantly improve their net income by utilizing depreciation of physical assets, such as buildings, and deducting mortgage interest and expenses.

A central theme of this book is to explain how investors can also defer and even eliminate capital gains on the sale of their real estate assets by taking advantage of Section 1031 of the Internal Revenue Code, which dates back to 1921.

Active versus Passive Investors

Active real estate investors have the greatest number of potential tax advantages. Active investors are defined as those who:

- Take direct responsibility for finding and financing their properties, including accepting any related loan guarantees

- Have a willingness to directly manage their properties, including handling tenant issues, dealing with unexpected emergencies, maintenance issues, accounting and tax matters, etc. (Or Property Management)

- Closely oversee the sale or refinancing of their properties when appropriate

By contrast, passive investors typically look for *mailbox* money and do not wish to be overly drawn into the day-to-day hassles of traditional real estate investments. The range of tax benefits available to passive investors is less than that of active investors, but still very significant. While many passive real estate investors began their investment careers as active investors, they tend to be older, more risk-averse, and primarily seek a reliable monthly income while leveraging estate planning options that can maximize wealth transfer to their heirs.

This book is focused on helping passive real estate investors better understand strategies that allow them to take maximum advantage of the tax code to safely increase their returns and, more specifically, how a relatively new real estate investment structure called the Delaware Statutory Trust (DST) may help them realize their personal investment objectives.

Overview of IRC Section 1031

The most common tax deferral strategies utilize treasury regulations that were first implemented with the passage of Internal Revenue Code 1031 (IRC 1031) in 1921. This legislation had two primary objectives, which remain relevant today: 1) To avoid unfair taxation of theoretical gains/losses in real property; 2) To encourage active reinvestment of proceeds in domestic real estate and thereby help to strengthen and stabilize property values.

With respect to unfair taxation, Congress recognized that:

". . . if a taxpayer's money is still tied up in the same kind of property as that in which it was originally invested, he is not allowed to compute and deduct his theoretical loss on the exchange, nor is he charged with a tax upon his theoretical profit. The calculation of the profit or loss is deferred until it is realized in cash, marketable securities, or other property not of the same kind having a fair market value."[2]

In other words, Congress recognized that it was fundamentally unfair to force an investor to pay taxes on a paper gain where the funds were still

---

2 H.R. Rep. No. 73-704, at 13 (1934), reprinted in 1939-1 (part 2) CB 554, 564.

a part of an ongoing investment in similar types of income-producing real estate assets. This objective encouraged real estate investment by allowing investors to keep their funds tied up in successive properties to avoid taxes if they did not cash out and take possession of their deferred gains. So, often starting with a single-family income property, real estate investors are free to trade gains upon sale into a duplex, then a small apartment, and possibly later into a shopping center, without paying any taxes if all gains are reinvested. Taxes only become due when assets are sold and the investor chooses to take control of the funds rather than reinvest them in another property.

The second objective that remains very relevant today is to encourage greater investment in the United States versus redeploying funds overseas. By providing incentives to invest in U.S. real estate, property values will tend to increase, leading to increased taxes that will be realized from rising property incomes (versus gains, which are deferred). Investors who sell U.S. assets lose their tax deferral status if those funds are reinvested in foreign real estate.

IRC 1031 will be covered in much more detail in Chapter 2.

Tenant in Common Investments

Throughout the twentieth century, 1031 Exchanges were generally limited to investments in wholly owned properties. In 2002, the introduction of Revenue Procedure 2002-22, also referred to as IRC 2002-22, granted investors an option to invest in fractional or co-ownership of real estate, which led to an explosive growth of 1031 Exchange transactions between 2002 and 2007. These investments were structured as a form of Tenant in Common (TIC) ownership, allowing up to 35 individual investors to pool funds and purchase larger institutional-class real estate assets. Unfortunately, the demand for these types of investments became overheated, and investors often became willing to invest in properties at prices above fair market value.

Lenders also contributed to the growth of TIC investments by offering loans on overpriced assets and then creating financial derivatives that combined multiple loans and resold them as high-grade investment vehicles to large institutions.

The Great Recession of 2008–2009 led to several negative consequences that all but eliminated the TIC structure, except in certain limited applications. The decline in rents triggered by the recession resulted in cash-flow shortfalls that many properties were unable to sustain. Many TIC owner groups were not able to contribute additional funds, thereby causing properties to go into a mortgage default followed by foreclosure and loss of all owner equity.

Even those properties that survived the recession suffered from a loss of value and were unable to provide anticipated owner distributions, creating frustration among investors, especially retired owners who invested in TICs as a means of generating retirement income.

With the failure of many of these TIC properties, lenders were forced to come to terms with flaws in the TIC structure and the consequences of their overly liberal lending policies, and they stopped funding most new TIC programs. Lenders are now very hesitant to lend to TIC investment property structures where there are more than a few investors, so investors seeking similar types of fractional passive investments need to consider other options.

The Delaware Statutory Trust

A trust is an arrangement whereby a third party, called a *trustee*, holds specified assets on the behalf of others who are designated as beneficiaries. The Delaware Statutory Trust (DST) is a specific type of trust that is generally set up to manage trust activities related to real estate assets. Although the trust structure for holding properties dates back to the sixteenth century,[3] the DST was first recognized as a legal entity for holding property after the passage of the Delaware Statutory Trust Act in 1988. In August 2014, the Internal Revenue Service published Internal Revenue Bulletin 2004-33, which ruled that:

---

3 https://en.wikipedia.org/wiki/English_law

"A taxpayer may exchange real property for an interest in the Delaware Statutory Trust described above without recognition of gain or loss under §1031, if the other requirements of §1031 are satisfied."[4]

This ruling created an alternative structure to the TIC structure described earlier, allowing passive investors to acquire and hold fractional interests of real estate assets that are afforded the full benefits of a 1031 Exchange, both upon purchase and sale. For reasons that are covered in significant detail in this book, the DST structure has become the preferred investment structure for passive investors seeking 1031 Exchange benefits.

Summary

In this introductory section, I have introduced the concept of tax-advantaged investments in real estate and provided a brief overview of the major tax provisions that have allowed investors to achieve higher net returns on real estate investments, including IRC 1031, IRC 2002-22, and IRC 2002-33.

Throughout the remainder of this book I will focus on providing the reader with practical information on the 1031 Exchange and explain factors as to why investors who seek real estate investments with minimal management responsibilities are increasingly investing in assets structured as a DST.

---

4 http://www.irs.gov/irb/2004-33_IRB/ar07.html

CHAPTER

2

THE 1031 EXCHANGE

In this chapter, I will present a pragmatic overview of the 1031 Exchange process, including several examples that will illustrate how the rules apply to typical transactions. As discussed in Chapter 1, the 1031 Exchange rules and guidelines date back to 1921, and several amendments have since been made to the original legislation. I will cut through the legalese of numerous related regulations and underscore the most useful nuts and bolts of information that is meaningful to the average investor.

Section 1031 of the Internal Revenue Code (IRC) is a fantastic piece of tax law that allows an investor to defer the capital gains or losses taxed on the sale of certain types of real estate investments, i.e., property that is held for productive use in a trade or business. Other forms of property such as stocks, bonds, personal possessions, etc., are excluded. The properties that are exchanged must be of a *like-kind* or have a degree of similarity, although the rules of what is considered *like-kind* are quite broad. For example, single-family income properties can be exchanged for retail, commercial office, or storage properties, and vice versa.

Simply put, Section 1031 of the IRC allows an investor to defer tax liabilities, provided they exchange into another business-use property investment[5].

---

5 Qualifying business-use properties can be any property or asset that is acquired and held for income production (rental or leasing activities) or for growth in value (capital appreciation). Properties held for investment do not

The reason that Section 1031 is so powerful is because the tax liability is substantial if an investor decides to cash out of an investment property. In California, for example, investors who decide to sell an investment property can face a blended state and federal tax rate that averages from 33% to 35%. Let's break that down.

Taxes Due Upon the Sale of Real Estate Investment Properties

Figure 2.1

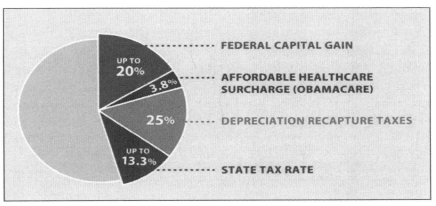

As a real estate owner, you're going to pay taxes at the federal level. If you happen to live in states with state income taxes, you're also going to pay taxes at the state level. Some states, like Florida and Texas,[6] have no applicable state tax obligations, but most of the states around the country do. If you happen to reside in one of those states, you are going to pay state taxes. Upon sale of real estate, you again pay taxes at the federal and state levels.

Currently, the federal capital gains tax is either 15% or 20%, depending on your income. In addition, you are also obligated to pay a 3.8% net

---

need to produce income or cash flow. They only need to be held for investment in order to qualify for 1031 Exchange treatment.

6 The seven states with no personal income tax are Alaska, Florida, Nevada, South Dakota, Texas, Washington, and Wyoming.

investment tax, known as the Obamacare or Medicare tax. This tax is subject to your income and kicks in if your adjusted gross income is over $250,000.

Another federal tax that a lot of people forget about is the depreciation recapture tax. It is the highest of all the individual taxes and is currently at a 25% rate. The depreciation recapture tax is simply a tax on the total amount of depreciation that you have taken over the life of your investment. All investment in business-use property has associated depreciation.

Depreciation Recapture Example

Residential rental properties generally are depreciated over 27.5 years, meaning that the tax code allows you to deduct a loss of value due to the growing age of your property, regardless of whether your property is increasing or decreasing in value over the same period (what a deal!). Owners of income real estate can offset the taxes due from property income by subtracting the allowed annual depreciation of building components of the property (but not the land) divided by 27.5.

For example, if your property costs $425,000 (price plus improvement costs), and $300,000 is the cost associated with the building portion of the property (excluding land), you may take an annual depreciation deduction of about $10,909 ($300,000/27.5). The depreciation deduction can offset rental income and along with other deductions, such as repairs, interest, and insurance, may result in reducing your taxable income to zero. Depending on your income, you can also deduct up to $25,000 of losses from your ordinary income. Thus, depreciation can provide substantial benefits to real estate investors that are not available on many other common forms of investment such as stocks, bonds, certificates of deposit (CDs), etc.

There is, however, the *rest of the story*. Unless you are doing a 1031 Exchange at the time you sell your investment property, you must *recapture* any depreciation you've taken (or could have taken) when you sell your property. The portion of your gain that is equal to the amount of depreciation you've previously taken is taxed at 25%, which is even higher than the highest capital gains rate.

Going back to our example, assume you purchased a rental property for $425,000. During the time you own the property, let's assume you depreciate $25,000 as per IRS rules, and then sell the property for $485,000. At sale, your adjusted basis in the property is $425,000 less $25,000, or $400,000. Your sales price of $485,000 less your adjusted basis of $400,000 will result in a taxable gain of $85,000. Because your gain of $85,000 exceeds the amount of depreciation taken ($25,000), the depreciation recapture rule will apply.

Thus, your tax will be $6,250 ($25,000 x 25%) + $9,000 ($60,000 x 15%[7]), or $15,250.

If you decide to sell that property rather than do a 1031 Exchange, you may incur a depreciation recapture tax liability of tens or even hundreds of thousands of dollars. Depreciation recapture tax is something that a lot of our investors forget about, but it is often the highest tax you will end up paying.

State Taxes

For those of us who are fortunate enough to live in California, we are painfully aware that the state of California is the highest tax collector in the country, taking anywhere from 9.3% to 13.3% of your total gains, in addition to the taxes owed to Uncle Sam. If you reside in California or if you're selling property in California (even if you do not live in California), you are expected to pay 9.3-13.3% in tax. Unlike federal government taxes, this tax is not split it up into a bunch of different taxes.

When all is said and done, if you're going to cash out of your property rather than do a 1031 Exchange, you can safely assume that up to 33-35% of your total gains will go in paying taxes. For many of our clients, that tax liability is in the tens or hundreds of thousands of dollars, leaving them to face several seven-figure tax liabilities.

---

7 The capital gains rate may be as high as 20% depending on your income.

Pay Taxes or Keep Your Money Working for You?

Should you pay taxes or keep your money working for you? Sounds like a no-brainer, right? While there is a case for paying taxes and not seeking a 1031 Exchange (e.g., no time or interest in finding a replacement property, immediate need for cash, etc.), I am constantly surprised by the large number of real estate investors that I encounter in our business who opt to pay taxes without giving any serious consideration to alternatives that could yield a much more favorable outcome. Let's look at the big picture.

If you decide to defer your tax liability and keep your money in your pocket instead of giving it to the government, you're able to use that money to leverage into bigger and better investments with bigger and better returns. Effectively, you're saying to the government, "Instead of giving my money to you, I'm going to keep my money working for me right now." You get to leverage your money to get into bigger and better properties. You're going to be building wealth much more quickly than if you cash out and pay taxes.

Remember, a third or more of your money could go to pay taxes. If you keep that money and put it to work for you, you're going to realize bigger and better returns much more quickly.

Figure 2.2

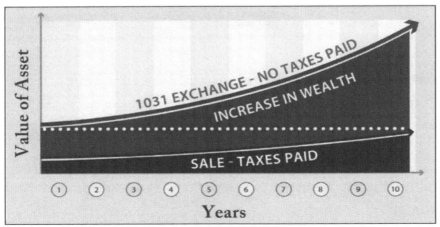

The ability to forgo paying taxes and instead reinvest proceeds into another income-growing property is one of the best wealth creating options available in the United States. Money that is spent paying taxes is lost forever. When your proceeds are reinvested, you will gain additional monthly income, buy larger and hopefully more profitable properties, and realize greater gains when those properties are eventually resold.

Swap Until You Drop

If those benefits are not sufficiently compelling, there is another huge benefit to those investors who plan to pass assets along to their heirs. The phrase *swap until you drop* means that your heirs can inherit your appreciated real assets and not pay *any* taxes whatsoever at the time they take title. *Yes, you read that correctly!* If they wish, they can imme-diately sell your appreciated assets after they take title and pay *no taxes* whatsoever. If they choose to continue to hold the assets for future ben-efits, their tax basis will be reset to fair market value on the day that the property is inherited from your estate, and will only be liable for future gains from that day forward.

When you pass on, the basis in the property steps up to fair market value for your heirs. Most readers will probably nominate their children as their heirs, but you don't have to. It could be anybody. You could nom-inate, for example, me. I will gladly be your heir! If you're going to pass away and you've got a $5 million apartment building that you own, the day that you pass, I will inherit that property. My basis in that property steps up to fair market value, which is $5 million. If I own a property for $5 million or I go out and sell a property for $5 million and my basis in that property is $5 million, I have a $0 tax liability.

Getting a step up in basis for your heirs is a fantastic way to eliminate tax liabilities that you've been deferring over a lifetime of investing, including any depreciation recapture benefits that you may have used to shield your past income from taxes. Many of our clients use this strat-egy. It's so common in our industry that I call it the three Ds of investing. You're going to defer, defer, and then die. Then your heirs are going to benefit from that step up in basis.

Swap until you drop strategies are widely used as one of the most potent estate-planning tools available to help preserve appreciated assets for the full benefit of one's heirs. If you are unfamiliar with this technique, please take the time to talk to your tax advisor or estate planner to better understand how this may apply to your situation, especially if you plan to leave assets to family and other heirs when you pass. *Swap until you drop* is a major exception to the adage that there is nothing as certain as death and taxes, as this strategy will at least help you avoid one of those certainties.

What Happens if I Decide to Cash Out?

One of the very important things to note when you're dealing with 1031 Exchanges is that you are deferring your tax liability. This means that you're simply kicking the can down the road. Unless you take advantage of a *swap until you drop* strategy, you're not necessarily getting out of paying taxes. If you do a series of exchanges and then stop exchanging, you are going to have to pay taxes on *all* your accumulated deferred gains plus taxes owed for any depreciation recapture benefits. Several of our clients who have done five or ten exchanges over a lifetime of investing and cashed out of their properties are now facing substantial tax liabilities.

The best way for strategic investors to avoid paying that potential tax liability is to simply never cash out of their properties. *You simply don't sell.* You own real estate until you die. Before you pass, you can plan accordingly to allow your heirs to benefit fully from the accumulated real estate wealth that you have created.

If the burdens of active real estate management become more than you can comfortably tolerate as you grow older, you can reinvest in more passive real estate options, such as DSTs, and shift the management burden to others.

Requirements for a 1031 Exchange

The first requirement for a 1031 Exchange is that you obviously must exchange into another property. The IRS provides guidelines on what type of properties that you can exchange into.[8] The government basically says that you can exchange into any property that's used for investment or business purposes, but it must be *like kind*. This confuses a lot of our investors. Some clients call us and they ask, "Well, if I sell a two-unit building, do I have to go out and buy another two-unit building?"

Fortunately, that's not the case. The like-kind requirement is broad and includes just about any type of real estate as long as it is used for business or investment purposes. They fall into two broad categories—*active investments* and *managed investments*.

Figure 2.3 [COMPOSITION: Please set the following lists (highlighted) side-by-side as a figure.]

Active Investments

- Residential
    - Single-Family Homes (rented)
    - Vacation Rentals (must meet criteria)
    - Apartment Complexes
    - Condominiums (rented)
- Commercial Office and Retail Properties
- Raw and Agricultural Land
- Mineral, Water, or Development Rights

Managed Investments

- Tenant in Common (TIC)
- Delaware Statutory Trust (DST)

As the title suggests, active investments consist of those real estate properties where the investor is primarily responsible for the following:

- Finding suitable properties

---

8 https://www.irs.gov/uac/Like-Kind-Exchanges-Under-IRC-Code-Section-1031

- Sourcing financing and accepting any loan guarantees
- Ongoing hands-on management
- Assuming added property liability and management risks
- Determining and executing exit strategies, including sale or refinance
- Accounting and tax reporting

While many of these responsibilities can be delegated, (e.g., you can hire a real estate broker to help find suitable properties, you can hire a management company to oversee your property, etc.) an active investment property requires the owner to be ultimately responsible for many aspects of property ownership, including many of the related liabilities. Owners of active investments should also be prepared to commit significant time to overseeing their properties, including dealing with unforeseen emergencies that might occur over the ownership cycle.

Managed investments are those that are sourced by a third party (sometimes referred to as a *sponsor*) who also takes on a primary role in managing, financing, assuming property liability risks, determining exit strategies, and providing property accounting and tax reporting. The income derived from these investments requires little to no incremental time on the part of the investor, and is typically paid out by the sponsor in the form of monthly distributions (often referred to as *mailbox* money). Such investments offer passive income. The clear majority of managed investments are offered to multiple investors, who each acquire a fractional interest in the property.[9]

As discussed in Chapter 1, the two ownership structures currently permitted by IRS that allow managed investments via a 1031 Exchange are the Tenant in Common (TIC) structure and the Delaware Statutory Trust (DST) structure. For reasons discussed elsewhere in this book, the DST

---

9 The types of managed investments being discussed here are not to be confused with real estate investment trusts (REITs) or real estate partnerships, because these structures are not considered like-kind investments and therefore are not available for a 1031 Exchange.

has emerged as the preferred structure, while TIC structures are rarely offered today (especially for larger numbers of investors).

A final point: You can exchange investments anywhere in the country, including all fifty states and Washington DC.[10] We have a lot of investors who sell in California to redeploy their equity in other states where better returns may be available. The tax code permits investors to sell and buy anywhere within the United States.

However, you cannot take your 1031 Exchange dollars from a sale of a U.S. property to buy property outside the country. If you sell in the United States, you have the flexibility to reinvest in any state in the country, but your investment cannot leave the United States.

Initiating a 1031 Exchange: Role of a Qualified Intermediary

The first step in initiating a 1031 Exchange is to take steps so that you do not have access to money from the sale of your property. To do so will void your ability to do a 1031 Exchange. The most effective way to accomplish this is by using a Qualified Intermediary (QI). The QI coordinates items related to the purchase and sale to meet 1031 Exchange requirements.

When you sell your existing property, the money will go to the QI, who will hold the funds in an escrow account. When you purchase your new replacement property, the QI will deliver the funds to the closing agent and the new property will be deeded over to you. The QI's fee will vary depending on the location and number of properties involved, but they will generally charge between $500 and $1,200 for a standard deferred exchange.

---

10 Temporary regulations issued in 2005 (T.D. 9194) allow exchanges to occur under certain circumstances between U.S.-based property and property located within the U.S. Virgin Islands, Guam, and Northern Mariana Islands. U.S. taxpayers may also do a 1031 Exchange from a foreign-owned property to another foreign-owned property, e.g., rental property in Canada can be exchanged for rental property in Costa Rica.

Function of the Qualified Intermediary

While the QI does not provide specific legal or tax advice to the investor who is planning to complete a 1031 Exchange, they typically provide the following services:

- Coordinate communications between the investor and their advisors to structure a successful exchange
- Prepare required documentation for the sold or relinquished property and the new replacement property
- Provide instructions to the escrow agent and provide documents to conclude the exchange
- Place the funds in an insured bank account pending the completion of the exchange[11]
- Provide documents to transfer replacement property to the investor and disburse exchange proceeds at the closing
- Hold identification documents of replacement properties submitted by the taxpayer
- Provide a written accounting of the exchange transaction for the taxpayer's records
- Provide a completed Form 1099 to both the taxpayer and the IRS detailing all proceeds/interest earned by exchange funds and paid to the taxpayer
- Prepare exchange documentation
- Hold relinquished property funds in a trust
- Ensure that the transaction complies with the guidelines of the tax regulations

I advise our clients to open their 1031 Exchange account as soon as a sales contract has been executed on the sale of a property. It is important to begin this process early because there are many

---

11 Some QIs will offer clients an option to place their funds in an interest-bearing account for the benefit of the client.

moving parts. The QI has a lot of people whose actions they need to coordinate. They've got to prepare documents and get various people to sign them. Additionally, it gives the QI plenty of time to review your transaction.

In a worst-case situation, if you are nearing the end of your 45-day identification period, an experienced QI can get the exchange account set up and have your documents prepared the day before you close. However, such a tight timeframe does not always work to the best interest of the investor and should be avoided. What's most important is that you get the QI involved before you close escrow. Once you've closed, it is then too late to engage a QI to complete an exchange.

Strangely, in this highly-regulated society that we live in, QIs are not regulated by any governmental bodies. They are not required to qualify for any licenses or ongoing continuing education. Therefore, it is relatively easy for any individual to get into the business.

 The problem is that when an exchange is opened, at some point, significant monies will need to be transferred from your sale escrow directly to an account managed by your selected QI.[12] There have been cases where unscrupulous QIs have secretly invested clients' monies into questionable and highly speculative investments without their knowledge, and some have even stolen funds outright and then disappeared.

Therefore, investors need to be very selective in choosing a QI and make sure they are dealing with a person who has a significant track record as well as impeccable credentials. Many excellent QIs are affiliated with large-title companies, banks, or insurance companies. Such an affiliation is a very important qualifier; however, the experience of the individual you select should also weigh heavily on your decision because the process of successfully completing an exchange can be complex, with many opportunities for mistakes that can potentially result in a reversal of previously claimed benefits in addition to stiff fines. You do not want to select a QI who is learning on your nickel!

---

12 You are not allowed to take possession or have any control of funds that earmarked for a 1031 Exchange. To do so is termed *constructive receipt* and results in the loss of exchange options.

Our firm works with QIs across the United States and would be pleased to provide referrals upon request.

1031 Exchange Timing Rules

Figure 2.4

| 0 | Identification Period | **45** Days | Exchange Period | **180** Days |

One of the most important elements of the 1031 Exchange process is that you must complete your 1031 Exchange on time. The government requires that when you sell and close escrow on your relinquished property, you must go out and get your exchange done within 180 calendar days from the close of escrow. Keep in mind that the regulations count holidays and weekends as part of the allowed timeline. If your 180th day happens to fall on a Sunday, you had better make sure that you get your exchange done by the Friday before because it may not be possible to close a sale on a weekend or holiday.

There are no extensions to the timeframe. You can't just call up the IRS and say, "Hey, I wasn't able to go in and close on day 180 so I need an extra week or two." The IRS is not forgiving when it comes to this specific rule, and a total of 180 days should be plenty of time to get your exchange done. Most of our investors do not have a problem with the 180-day time frame.

Our investors are, however, far more worried about day 45. When you are doing a 1031 Exchange, day 45 is very important because it is the last day that you must identify the replacement property (or properties) that you plan on buying. The IRS requires that you identify your exchange properties by filling out an identification letter no later than day 45. You formally nominate your potential replacement properties on the identification letter, and then are required to buy properties from that list. It is very important to understand that you cannot change your list after you submit the identification letter. Day 45 is very important.

To avoid the consequences of late identification, I recommend that investors don't wait until day 45. Many of our clients are in contract to buy replacement property as soon as they know that they are selling. Some of our clients line up replacement properties in advance of closing so that as soon as their property is sold, they purchase and close on their replacement property. Obviously, that doesn't work for everybody, and if you do need time to find a replacement property, you have 45 days.

Consequences of Bending the Rules

When stressing the importance of adhering to these dates, occasionally a client will make a comment such as, "Oh, come on, Paul, I have an exchange accommodator who will allow me to be more flexible on dates or even allow me to backdate agreements if needed."

Here's our standard response: The tax law is the tax law. The tax law states that you need to identify or nominate all your exchange properties by no later than day 45. If you don't follow the tax law, you don't have a valid exchange. In the past, there were friendly accommodators who might take a backdated letter. There are important and detrimental reasons why we don't see accommodating accommodators anymore.

First, of course, it's tax fraud. Second, beginning in 2012, a growing number of states, including California, have made audits of 1031 Exchanges one of their top priorities. Not only did the tax authorities step up their audits of individuals doing 1031 Exchanges, they went further and started auditing 1031 Exchange accommodators. Most of the major exchange accommodators across the United States are now subject to an audit of their practice.

For these reasons, it is now very rare that any QI from a reputable firm is willing to accept a backdated letter because the stakes are simply too high. A QI is only making a few hundred dollars for each transaction, and one bad deal can result in far greater liabilities, thereby removing any temptation to be dishonest.

To put it simply, bending the 1031 Exchange demining rules is a criminal offense. There are many cases where people have had exchanges reversed and have been ordered to pay heavy fines, and where the guilty intermediaries were subject to criminal federal prosecution.[13]

Let's move on to discuss the nuts and bolts of a 1031 Exchange.

1031 Exchange Examples

If you have done many 1031 Exchanges, you are free to skip this section, which covers basic examples of how exchanges work. However, for those readers who have not recently completed an exchange or are learning about the 1031 Exchange process for the first time, the information in this section is a good primer and demonstrates the key points of ensuring a successful 1031 Exchange.[14]

In general, for an exchange to work, the following three things must be equal or greater:

1. The net purchase price versus the net sale price

2. The net equity in the replacement property versus your relinquished property

3. The debt in the replacement property versus your relinquished property some of which can be replaced with new cash outside of the exchange) *How Much?*

Failure to meet these requirements can result in added taxes owed or what is commonly referred to as *boot*.[15]

---

13 *Dobrich v. Commissioner*, TC Memo 1997-47.

14 The examples in this section have been simplified for instructional purposes to illustrate key points. Please consult with your tax specialist when assessing tax consequences.

15 *Boot* is an old English term that refers to something that is given in addition to something else. In a 1031 Exchange, boot is additional money or value received.

To defer 100% of your tax liability, you need to consider several important items. First, you must purchase enough real estate to satisfy your exchange requirement, and if you don't want to pay any taxes, you must purchase property of equal or greater value compared to what you've sold. For example, if you sell a property for a net sales price of $1 million, you're going to have to buy a property valued at $1 million or more to defer taxes.

Note that we are discussing net sales price. Net sales price is important when we're talking about exchange properties because non-recurring closing costs, including commissions, title expenses, and transfer taxes, can be deducted from the gross sales price, resulting in your net sales price. It's the net sales price that you must replace with a new property.

The next thing to keep in mind is that you must replace all your cash (or your equity) in the property. When you sell a property, you will obviously pay your expenses. If you have any debt, the debt is going to be paid off, and the remaining cash balance is your equity. That equity will be transferred into the 1031 Exchange account set up by the QI and will be held until you are ready to purchase a replacement property. If you purchase property equal or greater in value and you spend all your cash, i.e., you invest all your available equity, you will defer 100% of your taxes.

The last item to consider is that there is a debt component in most sales transaction that will need to be replaced. Some people will tell you that you must always replace your debt, and while that's not necessarily true, most people do it. When you buy a new property, if you had debt on the one you sold, you're generally going to obtain a new loan on the replacement property you buy, although cash out of pocket can replace any debt requirement.

If you would simply like to contribute a bunch of cash to your 1031 Exchange, that's fine. You don't necessarily have to match debt or take on additional debt. Because most of our clients sell properties that have debt on them, they will replace the debt when they buy a replacement property, although this is not necessarily required. In our experience, nine out of ten investors will replace the debt rather than contribute additional cash.

Now that you understand the basic rules, let's cover several examples that will help you better understand how the rules apply in various situations.

Example 1: 100% Tax Deferral and No Boot Owed

Figure 2.5

Relinquished Property		Replacement Property	
Sales Price	$200,000	Purchase Price	$190,000
Escrow Expenses	$10,000	Exchange Proceeds	$90,000
Debt Payoff	$100,000	New Debt	$100,000
Exchange Proceeds	$90,000	Remaining Boot	$0
Result: No boot received since investor has reinvested all exchange proceeds into replacement property of equal value to the net sales price of the relinquished property (i.e., sales price less exchange expenses).			

Our first example shows a transaction that would result in a 100% tax deferral and no payment of any taxes. We start this transaction by selling a property for $200,000. Next, we are going to pay selling expenses of $10,000, and finally, we are going to pay off the $100,000 loan on the property. After completing that portion of the transaction, we have exchange proceeds or cash available of $90,000.

Remember, when we do our 1031 Exchange, we must reinvest that cash by purchasing a property equal to or greater in value to avoid paying taxes. Our net sales price on the relinquished property was $190,000, consisting of $90,000 in net exchange proceeds and $100,000 in debt. In this example, we purchased a replacement property for $190,000, reinvested all our exchange proceeds, and obtained a new loan equal to your old loan of $100,000. Congratulations! we have succeeded in concluding a 100% tax-deferred 1031 Exchange!

Example 2: Taxable Boot from Less Debt

Figure 2.6

Relinquished Property		Replacement Property	
Sales Price	$200,000	Purchase Price	$180,000
Escrow Expenses	$10,000	Exchange Proceeds	$90,000
Debt Payoff	$100,000	New Debt	$90,000 (less debt)
Exchange Proceeds	**$90,000**	**Remaining Boot**	**$10,000**
Result: The investor has $10,000 of taxable boot since there has been a trade down in value from the relinquished property to the replacement property. The trade down is caused by the investor taking on $10,000 less debt on the replacement property ("mortgage boot").			

In Example 2, we will look at the consequences of putting less debt on the replacement property. Like our first example, we start the exchange process by selling a property for $200,000. After selling expenses of $10,000, we have exchange proceeds of $90,000 sitting in our 1031 Exchange account. In this situation, we bought a replacement property with a purchase price of only $180,000.

This new property value is less than our relinquished property. The net sales price on the sold or relinquished property was $190,000 ($90,000 in net sales proceeds plus $100,000 of debt). We decided to buy a property for $180,000, consisting of our full exchange proceeds of $90,000 and a smaller loan of $90,000 versus our previous loan of $100,000. This is not the end of the world and does not disqualify the entire exchange by going down in value. We simply pay taxes on the difference, which in this case is a $10,000 gain due to less debt being taken on the replacement property.

Taxes owed in this example would be approximately as high as 35% of the gain, or $3,500. Taxes are owed in this example even though no additional cash came out of the transaction, and we would need to pay the owed taxes out of pocket. Once that check goes to the government, it is gone for good and the value of our estate is reduced accordingly. Again, this is not a terrible outcome because most of potential tax that would have been owed[16] is deferred and may ultimately be avoided

---

16 Keep in mind that the owed taxes are not just on the $90,000 gain in this example, but also on recapture of previous depreciation benefits on this

altogether if we decide to *swap until you drop* and pass the assets along to our heirs.

Example 3: Boot Offset with Extra Cash

Figure 2.7

Relinquished Property		Replacement Property	
Sales Price	$200,000	Purchase Price	$190,000
Escrow Expenses	$10,000	Exchange Proceeds	$90,000
Debt Payoff	$100,000	New Debt	$90,000 (less debt)
		Additional Cash	$10,000
Exchange Proceeds	$90,000	Remaining Boot	$0
Result: No boot. Even though the investor has taken on debt that is $10,000 less than the debt paid off on the sale of the relinquished property, the "mortgage boot" is offset by the investor paying an additional $10,000 towards the purchase price for the Replacement Property. In other words, the investor has offset the mortgage boot with additional cash paid.			

In Example 3, we are going to solve the problem that was created in Example 2 caused by taking less debt on our replacement property. In this example, we are going to add additional cash to the transaction to offset the reduction in debt. When first laying out the three basic exchange requirements at the beginning of this section, recall that one of the requirements is that we have equal or greater debt in the replacement property (some of which can be replaced with new cash outside of the exchange).

In this example, we are taking steps to avoid paying any taxes by investing an additional $10,000 in new cash into our replacement property. Through adding new cash to the transaction, we are buying enough real estate to satisfy our exchange requirement. That is, we are selling a property for a net sales price of $190,000, consisting of $90,000 in net proceeds and $100,000 in debt, and investing in a replacement property using $90,000 in net exchange proceeds, $90,000 from a new loan,

---

and all other previous exchanges that have preceded this exchange. The tax consequences of not doing an exchange could therefore be much larger than appears from this simple example, and the small amount of boot owed could be relatively inconsequential.

and $10,000 in new cash for total of $190,000. This results in an even exchange and a 100% tax deferral.

It is worth noting that this transaction only requires $6,500 in new money relative to Example 2, not the full $10,000. Why? Recall that in Example 2 we would need to come out of pocket to pay about $3,500 in owed taxes. Relative to Example 2, Example 3 would only require an additional $6,500 to eliminate the full tax burden.

Example 4: Taxes Owed Due to Cash Withdrawn

Figure 2.8

Relinquished Property		Replacement Property	
Sales Price	$200,000	Purchase Price	$190,000
Escrow Expenses	$10,000	Exchange Proceeds	$80,000 (not all proceeds used)
Debt Payoff	$100,000	New Debt	$110,000 (new debt is greater)
Exchange Proceeds	$90,000	Remaining Boot	$10,000
Result: The investor has $10,000 of taxable cash boot since the investor utilized only $80,000 of the $90,000 of Exchange Proceeds. While the investor can offset mortgage boot by paying additional cash, the investor cannot offset cash boot with additional debt on the replacement property.			

In Example 4 we have a case where some taxes are owed due to not reinvesting all the available cash and instead taking some cash out of the exchange (hopefully to enjoy a rewarding vacation because of our successful investments!). We start this transaction in the same manner as our previous examples by selling our property for $200,000, retiring our $100,000 loan, and netting $90,000 in exchange proceeds after sales expenses. In this situation, we decided to take some cash out and, even though we bought a property worth the same as our relinquished property or $190,000, we didn't use all our cash.

Remember, our cash reinvestment needs to be equal to or greater than the $90,000 of net exchange proceeds coming out of our relinquished property. In this example, when we purchased our replacement property, we decided to keep $10,000 and only put down $80,000 of our potential exchange proceeds. To offset the $10,000 reduction in cash that was invested in the new property, we took on more debt. The cash that we took out is taxable.

Example 5: Summary Example

In this final example, we are going to walk through a more comprehensive transaction, introduce some additional concepts, and conclude by quantifying the significant advantages of a 1031 Exchange. Extra time spent studying this example and understanding the math will produce a better grasp of intricacies of the 1031 Exchange.

No discussion of the 1031 Exchange is complete without touching on the concept of basis. The *original basis* is simply your original purchase price. The amount that you originally paid for your property is split between land value and building value. Building value can be depreciated; however, land cannot be. Residential properties can be depreciated over 27.5 years, and non-residential properties can be depreciated over thirty-nine years.

Net-Adjusted basis is used to determine the amount of capital gain that you derive from a sale. It is also used to determine the amount that can be depreciated on a replacement property. *Net-Adjusted Basis* is calculated by taking the original purchase price, adding all capital improvements, and then subtracting total depreciation taken during your ownership period.

Let's begin this example by looking at the following changes in basis in owning a residential income property over twenty years.

Figure 2.9

Original Purchase Price	$2,000,000
Capital Improvements	$100,000
Depreciation Taken During Ownership Period	**($1,000,000)**
Net-Adjusted Basis	**$1,100,000**

Let's now presume that the property increased in value over the twenty-year ownership period to $6,000,000, and you have decided to sell it today. The capital gains calculation would be determined as follows:

Figure 2.10

Sales Price if Sold Today	$6,000,000
Net-Adjusted Basis (from above)	**($1,100,000)**
Closing Costs Related to the Sale	**($400,000)**
Capital Gain	$4,500,000

Carefully note the following because this is where many investors make mistakes:

The $4,500,000 capital gain consists of two separately taxed components. The first and often overlooked component is the $1,000,000 of depreciation recapture taken from the data in Figure 2.9, which is generally taxed at a rate of 25%. The second component is the remaining capital gain, subject to normal capital gains and Obamacare taxes, which are a function of your tax bracket and the state you live in and where the property is located.

Presuming that you are in the highest tax bracket, the remaining capital gain of $3,500,000 ($4,500,000 less $1,000,000 depreciation recapture) will be taxed at a long-term federal capital rate of 23.8%, which consists of a 20% long-term federal capital gain rate of 20% and a 3.8% Obamacare surtax. If you happen to live in California, you will also be obligated to pay a state tax of 13.3%.

Let's see how this all adds up:

Figure 2.11

Capital Gain	$4,500,000
Depreciation Recapture	**($1,000,000)**
Net Capital Gain	$3,500,000
Owed Taxes	
Tax on Depreciation Recapture (25% x $1,000,000)	$250,000
Federal Capital Gains Tax (20% x $3,500,000)	$700,000
Obamacare Surtax (3.8% x $3,500,000)	$133,000
California State Tax (13.3% x $3,500,000)	$465,500
Total Tax Liability	$1,548,500

Now let's look at the options of cashing out or reinvesting using a 1031 Exchange. For both scenarios, we will assume a loan balance at time of sale of $1,000,000. Therefore, the total cash proceeds available at time of sale would be calculated as follows:

Figure 2.12

Sales Price if Sold Today	$6,000,000
Payoff of Current Loan	**($1,000,000)**
Closing Costs Related to the Sale	**($400,000)**
Net Cash Proceeds from Sale	$4,600,000

The potential tax liability as a percentage of net cash proceeds would therefore be:

Figure 2.13

Net Cash Proceeds from Sale	$4,600,000
Total Tax Liability	$1,548,500
% of Potential Taxes Owed ($1,548,500/$4.6M)	**34%**
% of Cash Proceeds Available after Taxes	**66%**

Finally, let's complete this example by looking at a comparison of purchasing power with and without a 1031 Exchange. In both cases, let's assume that funds from the sale of your current property will be invested in a new property and that you will obtain a new loan at 70% of the new property's value.

If you choose to not do a 1031 Exchange, the maximum property value that you can acquire would be:

Figure 2.14

After-Tax Sales Proceeds ($4,600,000 less $1,548,500)	$3,051,500
Purchasing Power with a 70% Loan	**$10,171,666**

If you choose to do a 1031 Exchange, the maximum property value that you can acquire would be:

Figure 2.15

Net Sales Proceeds	$4,600,000
Purchasing Power with a 70% Loan	**$15,333,333**
Additional Purchasing Power with 1031 Exchange	**$5,161,667**
($15,333,333 less $10,171,666)	

By electing to do a 1031 Exchange rather than pay taxes, you can purchase a property approximately 50% more valuable, thereby adding significant value to your estate! This is obviously a far better option rather than reducing the value of your estate by the amount of taxes you otherwise would have paid. Unless the investor had a critical need for receiving the cash, it therefore makes much more sense to reinvest the funds via a 1031 Exchange.

Calculation of Tax Basis for the Replacement Property

Presuming that the investor decides to move forward and complete a 1031 Exchange, additional consideration must be given to the calculation of the tax basis of the replacement property. You may recall that the original purchase price of the property is the investor's original tax basis in the property.

Per IRS regulations, the replacement property's tax basis is determined using a calculation based on the adjusted basis of the relinquished property sold in the exchange:[17]

"The basis of the replacement property acquired must be increased (or decreased) by the amount of the gain (or loss) recognized on the transfer of the relinquished property."

While I encourage investors to rely on their CPAs and tax advisors for these calculations, here is a simplified example of determining the tax basis in the replacement property using the figures from Example 5:

Figure 2.16

Adjusted Basis of Relinquished Property	$1,100,000
Plus Loan on Replacement Property	$10,733,333
($15,333,333 less $4,600,000)	
Basis in Replacement Property	**$11,833,333**

Summary

Nearly a century after being introduced, the 1031 Exchange remains one of the most popular techniques used by investors to defer and

---

17 Treasury Regulation §1.1031(d)-1(e).

potentially avoid taxes that are due from the gains from business income real estate properties. Preferential treatment of depreciation and the ability to write off various ownership expenses, including mortgage interest, repairs, etc., also allows investors to benefit from a high level of net cash flow that may be derived from their properties.

As summarized in this chapter, completing a successful 1031 Exchange can be a complex process requiring the assistance of qualified third parties. While the benefits can be compelling, there are challenges that need to be considered: 1) finding suitable replacement properties within the required timeframes, 2) determining the actual amount of savings given other gains and losses that vary per situation, and 3) scrupulously following applicable rules to avoid negative tax audit consequences.

Because the 1031 Exchange is primarily applicable to business real estate investments, there are additional investor responsibilities that may require ongoing management and supervision and that may also be subject to market risks.

The remainder of the book will focus on utilizing the Delaware Statutory Trust ownership structure, which allows passive investors to take advantage of 1031 Exchange tax benefits.

3

THE DELAWARE STATUTORY TRUST

The Delaware Statutory Trust (DST) can solve the following issues faced by real estate investors:

- The market currently provides an annual income range of 4–6%, which can be partially shielded from income tax due to permitted tax deductions under the Internal Revenue Service (IRS) code

- Reduces many management responsibilities commonly faced by owners of income-producing real estate

- Provides pre-packaged property options that include due diligence information, track record of the sponsor/manager, and a fully approved loan (if financed)

- Provides access to institutional-quality properties with in-place management

- Permits investors to take full advantage of the 1031 Exchange tax deferral

- May be used in combination with other replacement property options to further reduce tax obligations

- Minimum investments can be as low as $25,000 for cash investors

- No requirement to qualify for the property loan

- Identification and investment can be completed in five days or less making DSTs ideal for 1031 Exchange investors who are running short of time to locate a replacement property

The remainder of this chapter will cover topics that have been requested by investors, attorneys, CPAs, and real estate professionals who are seeking to better understand DSTs. Not all topics will be relevant to all readers, so you are encouraged to skip through material that may not be applicable to your current situation.

Introduction

As discussed in Chapter 1, the concept of holding property in a trust dates back to sixteenth-century English Common Law. Typically, a trust is managed by a trustee as a fiduciary for the benefit of beneficiaries. The recognition of the trust structure as a formal legal entity affording certain legal rights and limited liability for participants did not exist until the enactment of the Delaware Statutory Trust Act in 1988. In 2004 the IRS published Internal Revenue Ruling 2004-86, which contained the following important clarifications that dramatically increased use of the DST structure by real estate investors:[18]

A) A DST is a legal entity, separate from their trustee(s), offering them limited liability.

B) A DST is identified as a trust for federal tax purposes, making it a pass-through entity that mitigates taxation for its trustee(s).

C) Real property that is held under a DST is eligible to use a 1031 Exchange, without the recognition of gain or loss, as long as the following seven restrictions (aka *The Seven Deadly Sins*) are met:

---

18 https://en.wikipedia.org/wiki/Delaware_statutory_trust

1. Once the offering is closed, there can be no future contributions of assets to the DST by either current or new beneficiaries.

2. The trustee cannot renegotiate the terms of the existing loans and cannot borrow any new funds from any party, unless a loan default exists because of a tenant bankruptcy or insolvency.

3. The trustee cannot reinvest the proceeds from the sale of its real estate.

4. The trustee is limited to making capital expenditures with respect to the property for normal repair and maintenance, minor nonstructural capital improvements, and those required by law.

5. Any reserves or cash held between distribution dates can only be invested in short-term debt obligations.

6. All cash, other than necessary reserves, must be distributed on a current basis.

7. The trustee cannot enter into new leases, or renegotiate the current leases, unless there is a need due to a tenant bankruptcy or insolvency.

Due to limitations related to lack of flexibility in negotiating new leases and adding new funds to properties, applications of the DST structure are generally limited to the following two tenant structures:

- Single-tenant triple net (NNN) properties where the tenant is responsible for all property costs under a long-term lease.

- A Master Lease structure whereby a Master Tenant, who is usually affiliated with the Sponsor of the DST program, subleases the property to other tenants. The Master Tenant is responsible for paying the full owed rent on the property and is also responsible for all repairs, maintenance, taxes, insurance, etc. In many ways, they fulfill a role similar to a single-tenant NNN property.

The Master Lease structure is recognized as a legally acceptable structure per DST and 1031 Exchange regulations. Its major benefit to investors is that properties that have ongoing leasing, such as apartments and other multi-tenant properties (e.g., office buildings, self-storage, retail, etc.), and that would be otherwise ruled out of being structured as a DST per #7 of the Deadly Sins summarized above can be successfully structured under a Master Lease arrangement and be in full compliance.

As compared to single-tenant NNN properties, the Master Lease structure may pose some additional risks that investors should consider:

- The Master Tenant entity may have less creditworthiness than a tenant in an NNN lease. The Master Tenant is not an ongoing business, and its ability to guarantee lease obligations will be closely related to its relationship to the Sponsor of the DST program.

- Master Lease structures require reserves that must be funded up front and possibly added to from ongoing operations. These reserves will be needed to pay certain expenses, such as lease renewals, maintenance, etc., to allow the property to successfully operate. If the reserves are not sufficient, the Master Tenant will need to draw on the resources of the Sponsor to provide needed funds.

Even in consideration of these potential risks, many investors are attracted to multi-tenant assets like apartments over single-tenant properties. Multi-tenant properties are usually better able to adjust rents to current market conditions because the underlying leases are of shorter duration than might be the case with a long-term NNN lease. This may be especially advantageous during inflationary cycles. Apartments have also tended to appreciate more than other assets during the most recent investment cycle post the 2008 recession.

DST versus Tenant in Common Investments

While DST investments have some common features with the Tenant in Common (TIC) structure, there are some very important differences that have caused most investors to prefer a DST over a TIC investment. Common features include the following:

1) Both structures permit fractional ownership of real estate with full 1031 Exchange tax deferral benefits, thereby allowing investors to combine their equity and purchase larger institutional-class assets that may be easier to manage and sell in the future.

2) Both structures also produce income that can be at least partially shielded through pass-through tax benefits.

3) Both types of investments are classified as securities and can only be offered and purchased through a licensed securities dealer. Real estate agents/brokers lacking securities licenses are unable to offer these structures to their clients.

Detailed below are the major differences between the DST and TIC structures.

Property Loans

One of the most attractive aspects of the DST is that individual investors do not need to qualify for any property loans or have any recourse from the lender if the property fails. The trustee and/or the sponsor company bears full responsibility for any loan guarantees.

Lenders also do not require that investors establish and maintain a separate limited liability company (LLC). Costs for maintaining LLCs can range up to $1,000 per year, so a DST investor is spared this expense.

 A TIC investment does require investors to submit financial statements to qualify as a borrower.

While most TIC loans are non-recourse to the borrowers, TIC investors are, however, subject to certain penalties (*bad boy carve-outs*) if they engage in specified prohibited actions, such as filing for bankruptcy.

Due to other issues associated with TIC structures (see below), in general, lenders are no longer making loans to properties structured as TICs. This has led to almost a total shutdown of new investments in the TIC structure.

Number of Investors

DSTs have no IRS-imposed limits on the number of investors. Thus, investors can purchase larger properties and invest with minimums as low as $25,000 for cash investors. By contrast, TIC investments are limited to a total of 35 investors. Minimums for TIC investments can range from as high as several hundred thousand dollars to one million dollars or more for larger assets.

Decision-Making

In general, all major decisions in a DST are made by the trustee.[19] Individual DST investors do not have decision-making rights and can neither make nor prevent decisions that can impact the property. The relationship of individual investors in a DST is like investments made in real estate investment trusts (REITs), mutual funds, or even stocks where the assets are managed by a professional team on behalf of the investors.

Individual investors in a TIC structure have the ability to make certain decisions that can impact other investors (e.g., firing a manager, disapproving a new lease, not agreeing to sell or refinance). These types of decisions in a TIC structure require unanimous approval of *all* investors,

---

19 Operational decisions are generally made by the Master Tenant.

so the disapproval of any one investor can have significant consequences on all other investors.

While the notion of having a degree of control can be appealing to TIC
investors, history has proven that the power to exercise negative votes
that conflict with the desires of other investors can potentially be very
damaging to the success of the investment.

The unanimity requirement for certain decisions in a TIC structure is one
of the main reasons lenders have generally suspended making loans to
such structures. Based on abuses and issues stemming from providing
a larger number of individuals with added control, lenders have concluded that this perceived investor benefit is a serious liability.

No Negative Consent

In many TIC agreements, there is a decision-making provision stating that
if an investor does not affirm a recommendation in writing, their non-re-
sponse will be treated as approval of the proposal. As with the issue of
unanimity discussed above, this *negative consent* provision common to
most TIC agreements was viewed as a benefit to investors. However, history has revealed many abuses, especially by predatory asset managers
who leverage this provision in a manner that is not favorable to owners.

Here is an example:

TIC managers earn significant fees through management, sales, and
leasing activities. Unscrupulous managers can take advantage of owners by sending out ballots with proposals that are favorable to the manager, such as the annual renewal of the management agreement, on
the day before a holiday period or before a long weekend, giving the
owners a shorter period to respond. Owners who do not check their
email are then surprised to learn that they have unintentionally voted
in favor of something favorable to the manager that is not in their best
interests—and they are unable to rescind their silent vote.

Like many other types of investments involving large groups of individuals, DST investors do not have any negative consent (or any other) voting
rights. The decisions are solely made by the trustee. Obviously, if the
trustee makes decisions that are not in the best interests of investors,

problems can arise in a DST as well. History has shown, however, that DST trustees make decisions that benefit their investors much more consistently. Evidence of this can be found in the virtual absence of lawsuits or damage claims by DST investors against their trustees.

In contrast to TIC managers, a DST trustee is held to a higher fiduciary standard, and the additional burdens of this role better align investor interests with those of the trustee, resulting in fewer conflicts.

No Time Limits on Management Agreement

Under the DST structure, the property manager typically stays in place for the full period of the investment. Generally, the sponsoring firm or an affiliate is the property manager, although this function may be delegated to a third-party manager. If the property is not managed well, investors do not have the option to terminate the manager except in extreme cases, e.g., bankruptcy, gross negligence, etc. Again, this type of limited management control is common to many forms of investment.

In a TIC structure, IRS guidelines mandate that management agreements are subject to annual renewal and that any one TIC investor can terminate the management agreement toward the end of each calendar year. Serious problems can arise if the manager is terminated, however, because without a replacement manager already in place, a technical loan default would be triggered per language in most TIC loan documents.

Another challenge is that the appointment of a replacement manager would need to be approved unanimously by all TIC owners and the lender. Without an approved successor manager in place at the time a current manager is terminated, some lenders have even taken the extreme position of appointing a receiver to manage the property.

While the annual renewal requirement was initially viewed to be a benefit to the TIC structure, in hindsight, this provision has created many issues for TIC owners.

Bankruptcy Remote

A bankruptcy remote entity is an ownership entity within an entire ownership group whose bankruptcy has little to no economic impact on other entities within the group. A bankruptcy remote entity is often a single-purpose entity (SPE).

The DST is a bankruptcy remote, so it contains provisions that prevent any investors' bankruptcy creditors from reaching the DST's property and gives the lender greater security so that it could foreclose on its first mortgage of the real estate. The only right that beneficiaries have relative to the trust is to receive distributions. These provisions are favorable to both investors and to the lender.

Required Documentation

The documentation that investors are required to complete to invest in a DST is much less burdensome than that required in a TIC investment. In most DST structures, investors will need to fill out a questionnaire confirming that they are an accredited investor[20] and that they understand the related risks of investing in real estate. Completing this documentation is generally painless, and sponsor representatives or financial advisors can assist if needed.

By contrast, in a TIC investment, the investor is also a borrower and needs to qualify for the underlying loan on the property. To qualify for the loan, significantly more documentation needs to be generated, including personal financial statements, bank records, etc. The TIC investor will also be required to sign up for loan guarantees that can be severe if certain loan covenants are not met.

---

20 With respect to individuals, an accredited investor needs to meet the following criteria: 1) earn an individual income of more than $200,000 per year, or a joint income with spouse of $300,000, in each of the last two years and expect to reasonably maintain the same level of income, or 2) have a net worth exceeding $1 million, either individually or jointly with his or her spouse, excluding personal residence.

No Loan Guarantees for DSTs

Sponsors of TIC investments are often quick to point out that loans on TIC properties are generally *non-recourse*, meaning that, if a property fails, the lender cannot go after the personal assets of the borrower. Notwithstanding this non-recourse description, the fine print in the loan documents will generally describe several so-called *bad boy* acts that, if undertaken by the borrower, may result in liability for owners to repay the loan from their personal assets.

There are two types of non-recourse guarantees in a TIC loan, often referred to as *carve-outs*. The most onerous of these results is the borrower being fully liable for the entire loan. Examples of these include:

- A borrower filing for bankruptcy or consenting to or facilitating an involuntary bankruptcy proceeding or receivership

- Failing to properly maintain the SPE that provides bankruptcy remote covenants contained in the loan documents (see below)

- Failing to allow inspections of the property by the lender

- Failing to deliver requested financial information to the lender

- Allowing a voluntary lien to encumber the property

- Transferring one's ownership interest in violation of the provisions of the loan document

The second type of non-recourse guarantee includes personal liability for acts or events limited to what the lender suffers. Examples include:

- Fraud or misrepresentation

- Gross negligence or willful misconduct

- Any environmental indemnification

- Misappropriation or conversion of insurance or condemnation proceeds, rents, or security deposits

- Failure to maintain required insurance

- Failure to pay real estate taxes

- Waste at the property, i.e., failure to adequately maintain the property

- Commission of a criminal act unrelated to the property

The most obvious conclusion for TIC investors in perusing this list of potential loan liabilities is that many of these items are subject to the performance of the property manager, not the owners. Yes, the TIC owners will potentially be held responsible for the lack of performance of their managers, even if they were not aware of such performance failures. So, the absence of loan liabilities of any sort related to property ownership is a huge differentiator in favor of the DST structure.

The table in Figure 3.1 provides a summary of key differences and advantages of DSTs versus TICs.

Figure 3.1

TIC vs. DST STRUCTURE		
TICs	**DSTs**	**DST Advantages**
Only 35 investors	Up to 499 investors	Provides access for more investors
Higher investment minimums	Lower investment minimums	Provides smaller investment amount
Up to 35 separate real estate closings	Lender only needs to make one loan because the DST owns 100% of the real estate	Provides simple and more efficient closing investment process (frequently 24-hour turn-around)
Each investor is required to have recourse (personal liability) with respect to "bad boy" and some environmental loan carve-outs	Loan carve-outs apply to sponsors, not investors	Provides investors protection against personal liability under loans
All major decisions require unanimous agreement by investors	Sponsor (as Trustee) is better equipped to deal with crises than 35 individual TICs	Provides the ability to act quickly when issues arise
Investors can be liable for the actions of their co-investors	Investors cannot cause a default on the entire loan	Provides investors greater security against rogue investors
Each investor must set up an individual LLC	Investors do not need separate LLCs	Provides a less complex structure for investors
Lender underwrites each investor	Lender does not underwrite the investors	Eliminates need for investors to provide tax returns to lenders

Case Study: Unlocking Your Investment Property's Trapped Equity

Many of the most successful real estate investors over the last two decades are those who invested in the booming housing market. With a rapidly growing economy and increased housing demand, many home owners have seen their properties dramatically increase in value. With the increase in value also comes a higher amount of equity retained in the investment. While this appreciation in value is a benefit for the investor, the challenge is that the equity gain in the investment (or *trapped equity*, as I refer to it) is not being put to work.

Consider the story of Mary and John, who bought a Bay Area home in the early 1980s for a whopping $125,000 with a $25,000 down payment. Since the time since of their purchase, Mary and John, both successful professionals, have moved into a new home with their ever-expanding family and are now renting their first house out to tenants. While John has always been handy regarding home repairs and Mary enjoys interacting with the various families that cycle through the property, they are approaching retirement and looking forward to traveling more while working less.

Their first home is now worth $1,400,000, with roughly $1,300,000 in equity after closing costs. The rent they receive from the property provides about $20,000 in annual pre-tax cash flow after all expenses. However they have exhausted the allowed depreciation benefits[21] and now have less after-tax income. John and Mary are wondering if there is a better solution to match their retirement and travel plans.

After considering various options, Mary and John decide to sell their rental property and complete a 1031 Exchange to move their sales proceeds into a small portfolio of DST properties that include net leased single-tenant retail properties and class A multifamily assets. Mary and John can now benefit from a diversified portfolio of institutional-grade real estate without the headaches and late-night calls associated with hands-on management. And what's better, they are utilizing the full power of the equity from their investment property and realizing an average of 5–7% annualized cash flow, which delivers about $75,000 in income that is mostly tax sheltered.

Because Mary and John have unlocked the trapped equity from their income property and put it to work, their new portfolio of real estate investments will be able to generate a higher amount of recurring income and provide them with both added income and time to more fully enjoy their retirement.

How Lenders View the DST

Benefits for Lenders

DSTs are structured in a manner that prevents potential creditors, lien holders, or judgments of any of the investors/beneficiaries from

---

21 Recall that you can depreciate the non-land value of your residential real estate investment over 27.5 years and reduce otherwise owed taxes in each year you claim depreciation. After 27.5 years of ownership, you can no longer claim this deduction and need to pay additional taxes.

impacting the investment property held in the trust. Lenders therefore have an easier path to foreclose on a property if loan obligations are not met.

Unlike the TIC structure, there is no requirement to renew the property management contract each year in a DST, so lenders have greater assurances that the property will be consistently managed without a management transition. Furthermore, lenders can rely on a professional manager to make all key property decisions and not be subject to dissenting owners who can block key decisions.

The individual investors or beneficiaries in the DST are not required to individually qualify for the loan, nor is their financial status a consideration for any loan on the property because they are not the borrowers. The DST is the borrower, and the trustee executes all the loan documents and is responsible for related loan obligations and any guarantees.

There is also reduced paperwork and monitoring for the lender because there is only one borrower and typically only one guarantor on a DST loan.

Finally, lenders do not need to monitor or approve transfers of DST interests between investors. This is a very important benefit if investors decide to sell their DST interests to others because the process of transferring interests is much easier and less costly due to the absence of lender approvals.

Risks for Lenders

DSTs are not immune to many of the standard ownership risks of real estate. Chief among these are market risks that are difficult to predict, including unexpected changes to the overall economy, submarket shifts (e.g., the impact of lower oil prices in Houston), interest rates, etc. Risks related to the borrower/sponsor are more straightforward to quantify and assess. Lenders consider the following risks when evaluating loans:

- The ability of the DST sponsor/manager to effectively manage and operate the property

- The track record and experience of the sponsor/manager in previous similar real estate investments with multiple investors

- The financial worthiness of the sponsor to handle unexpected problems that may arise during the ownership period

- Risk that the sponsor may abandon the property

It is fair to say that because many lenders were burned by TIC sponsors whose loans frequently went bad, today's lenders who make loans to DST sponsors apply higher underwriting standards before granting a loan. While DSTs for 1031 Exchanges have been in existence since 2004, very few DSTs have in fact failed to repay loans, whereas many TIC-owned properties have been unable to meet their debt obligations during the same period.

Typical Loan Requirements

To address the risks noted above, a lender will require, among other things, the following:

- The DST trust and a master tenant (if there is one) must each be a bankruptcy remote SPE entity. The lender's security is better protected relative to other loans that lack bankruptcy remote provisions because in the event of either or both entities filing for bankruptcy, the lender would be able to foreclose on the property without undue delays.

- The sponsor, loan guarantor(s), and any master tenant must have sufficient creditworthiness to qualify for the loan.

- Generally, the primary lease term must extend beyond the term of the loan.

- The property must have sufficient funds set aside at the onset of the investment to support all anticipated expenses that are not paid from operations.

- The trustee or sponsor will typically be required to retain a small interest in the DST trust.

- Large investors in the DST holding more than 25% ownership may need to submit additional financial documentation to assess their creditworthiness.

- The master tenant and any property manager must agree to subordinate their compensation to superior claims made by the lender.

- If an emergency capital requirement arises, there must be an operating agreement provision between the trustee and the investors that would allow the formation of a Springing limited liability company (LLC) (see below) to replace the DST structure and for the sponsor to become the managing member of the new LLC.

How a Springing LLC Protects Investors and Lenders

DST agreements commonly contain provisions that allow a trustee to convert the DST structure into an LLC if an unforeseen capital call is required. Recall that one of prohibited actions for a DST is that no further capital can be invested after the property is initially capitalized.[22]

What if an unexpected event occurs that requires significant fresh capital, e.g., early failure of a heating, ventilation, and air conditioning system; roof collapse; bankruptcy of a key tenant; etc.? If the trustee determines that significant loss of property value may occur unless additional external capital is invested, it can change the structure of DST into a limited liability company (LLC) (aka the *Springing LLC*), which has no

---

22 Limited capital can be contributed from ongoing operations without violating this provision, provided this is fully disclosed up front and is part of the approved operating plan for the property.

such prohibitions. This conversion may be quickly accomplished per Delaware law, which allows the conversion through a simple filing.

To provide added lender protection, the Springing LLC has the same bankruptcy remote provisions as the DST and allows the raising of additional funds, fresh financing, and other actions prohibited under the DST (the Seven Deadly Sins), such as renegotiation of the existing financing or entering new or modified leases. In addition, the typical language in the operating agreement allows the trustee or sponsor to become the managing member of the Springing LLC and will be responsible for making all critical decisions on a go-forward basis.

While proper use of the Springing LLC option can save an otherwise troubled property, investors may lose their ability to perform a 1031 Exchange out of the property when it is eventually sold. The conversion of a DST into an LLC may not be as serious as losing all of one's equity, although the consequences can result in significant tax liabilities upon sale due to recapture of past tax benefits.[23]

Structure of DSTs

A DST is classified as a security and is subject to certain securities laws. Today almost all DSTs are structured to be subject to Regulation D, which allows the DST to be exempt from full securities law registration. Regulation D is the most popular form of structuring private equity securities investments and is currently utilized to raise over $1.3 trillion annually.[24]

Regulation D (*Reg D*) has evolved since it was first introduced in the mid-1930s, and it now has two variations that are currently used for DSTs. These Reg D variations are referred to as Rule 506(b) and Rule 506(c). Both these rules have the following in common:

---

23 Some attorneys promote their ability to restructure properties that have exercised a Springing LLC option back into a tax-advantaged structure such as TIC prior to sale and therefore restore the ability of investors to complete another 1031 Exchange. We have not studied cases where this has been successfully tested.

24 https://www.sec.gov/news/speech/stein-sec-speaks-2016.html

- Offerings can only be sold to qualifying accredited investors or institutions by registered and licensed broker-dealers and securities agents. (Reg D offerings cannot be purchased through real estate brokers or agents unless those individuals are also properly licensed as securities dealers.)
- There is no limit on offering size.
- Companies must file the offering with appropriate state and federal agencies and provide ongoing reporting to government agencies.

The passage of the JOBS Act in 2012 led to several changes in securities laws that are intended to reduce regulation that had hindered job creation. One of these provisions was the introduction of the Reg D Rule 506(c) exemption that allows an issuer to engage in general advertising and solicitation of accredited investors for the securities offering. Permission for general advertising is very broad and can include use of the internet, radio, television, and other common forms of advertising, subject to specified disclosures that must accompany such advertising.

As with many types of legislation that offer apparent benefits, Rule 506(c) has a catch that has limited its broader use. Issuers that choose to structure their offerings under Rule 506(c) to be able to publicly advertise their offerings must take added steps to verify that investors who invest are, in fact, accredited. Accredited investors must provide proof to the issuer or an approved third-party verification firm that they meet accredited standards for income or net worth. In practice, the process of gathering proof of accreditation has proved to be time-consuming, and many potential investors are simply unwilling to submit the required documents. There are also harsh penalties for issuers who are unable to provide proof that all their investors meet the accreditation standards.

By contrast, Rule 506(b), which has been in effect since 1982, prohibits public advertising of private securities offerings. The benefit for the issuer is that investors do not need to submit proof of their accreditation status; issuers can rely on their investors' written statements and signed questionnaire that they are accredited.[25]

While public advertising for DSTs would undoubtedly increase investor interest, due to challenges in determining the accreditation status of investors who are publicly solicited, almost all DSTs today are structured under Reg D Rule 506(b). Investors seeking DST options will therefore need to contract registered broker-dealers to learn about the available offerings. I will discuss the process of how investors can source DST options in Chapter 4.

Purchase of DSTs are Governed by Securities Laws

Due to limited control by the investor and the role of the third-party manager/sponsor of the investment, federal rules mandate that the sale of DSTs is governed by securities laws. Several important consequences flow from this:

- DSTs can only be purchased through registered and properly licensed securities dealers.
- Real estate agents and brokers are not able to sell DSTs or receive any compensation that is based on the amount of funds raised.
- Securities dealers are forbidden to share any fees with individuals who are not also licensed as securities brokers. This includes prohibitions on providing finder's fees to unlicensed individuals.

Resale of DST Interests

Restrictions on the sale of DST interests structured under Reg D coupled with lack of an established secondary market are one of the downsides to investing in DSTs. While the process of reselling Reg D DST interests can be challenging and time-consuming, there are ways in which a resale of DST interests can be concluded.

---

25 https://www.sec.gov/info/smallbus/secg/general-solicitation-small-entity-compliance-guide.htm

A first step for an investor who wishes to resell their interests is to inform their securities representative of their desire to sell and set a minimum price they would accept. The securities representative will then contact the sponsor/trustee on behalf of the investor to initiate communications with other investors in the same DST to determine whether those investors who are already familiar with the asset have an interest in acquiring additional interests. Additional exposure can be provided to investors in other DSTs if interest in the same DST is not sufficient.

Because DST interests typically have an ongoing revenue stream, demand from other DST investors seeking income should not be difficult to develop. If needed, a discount might be offered by the seller, which would increase the rate of return and create further demand.

Regulation A+: The Future of DSTs?

Title IV of the JOBS Act of 2012 also introduced a revamped version of Regulation A, aka Reg A+, which I believe will have a significant impact on the future structure of DSTs. Before going further, I ask the reader for permission to make a shameless plug for my previous book, entitled *Regulation A+: How the JOBS Act Creates Opportunities for Entrepreneurs and Investors*, published by APRESS and available from many book outlets, including Amazon.[26]

Approved by the Securities and Exchange Commission (SEC) in June 2015, Reg A+ goes beyond Reg D in helping entrepreneurs and investors create more investment opportunities. Most significantly, Reg A+ permits public advertising to both accredited and non-accredited investors and does not require the onerous gathering of proof of the investor's accreditation status.

DSTs structured under Reg A+ can be readily advertised on public media channels and be available to a much larger pool of investors. Today only about 7% of the U.S. population qualifies as an accredited investor and

---

26 https://www.amazon.com/Regulation-Creates-Opportunities-Entrepreneurs-Investors/dp/1430257318/ref=sr_1_1?ie=UTF8&qid=1481676058&s-r=8-1&keywords=Regulation+A%2B%3A+How+the+JOBS+Act+Creates+Op-portunities+for+Entrepreneurs+and+Investors

is therefore eligible to invest in DSTs structured subject to Reg D securities exemptions.[27] DSTs structured under Reg A+ can be offered to all classes of investors, accredited and non-accredited, thereby opening a vastly larger market of investors who can realize benefits that were previously limited to only the wealthy.

Another advantage of the Reg A+ structure is that investor interests can be freely traded and resold without restriction. As noted above, one of the issues that cause concerns among DST investors is the lack of liquidity of their investments and the relatively long hold period before their invested equity is returned. This issue results from the fact that the current Reg D structure does not allow easy trading of Reg D securities. The sale and transfer process is cumbersome at best and, as a practical matter, is rarely completed. The lack of tradability also works against any interest from brokers in creating secondary markets to trade or resell DST interests.

Because Reg A+ DST interests can in theory be freely traded, I would expect to see a secondary market develop where DST interests would trade much like real estate investment trusts or bonds. They would provide a monthly dividend to the owners and then, like a bond, have equity returned when the property is sold. How the IRS may view this process remains to be seen, and it may be the case that some aspects of 1031 Exchange options upon sale may be altered due to increased tradability of ownership interests.

One of the potential drawbacks of using Reg A+ is that a new offering must be submitted for SEC approval, and no funds can be accepted by the sponsor until all comments from the SEC have been satisfied. In addition, each offering must include a mini-business plan and other related information that is required in the filing documents. In some cases, audited statements of prior history must also be included. Therefore, the process of initiating fundraising for a Reg A+ offering can be longer relative to a Reg D offering, which does not require prior approval from the SEC. However, the filing can also be initiated during the due diligence phase of acquiring a property and, under the guidance of

---

27 http://www.forbes.com/sites/devinthorpe/2014/07/15/sec-mulls-changes-to-accredited-investor-standards-18-crowdfunders-react/#ee4d7e436489

an attorney with solid Reg A+ experience, the approval could be concluded by the time the due diligence and the property acquisition has been completed.

Acquiring quality real estate is very often time-sensitive and sellers may lack tolerance for a delayed close, so most DST sponsors have been reluctant to jump into Reg A+ despite the significant potential benefits. I believe that it is only a matter of time before DSTs are offered in a Reg A+ structure, and that the resulting heightened demand will create rapidly growing acceptance of this structure.

There are some trade-offs that a DST sponsor must consider and a Reg A+ structure would not be a fit for all types of DST options. But its growing use in the future is very likely to greatly expand both the visibility and growth of DSTs.

Summary

In this chapter, I have summarized the key aspects of the DST structure and compared it to the previously used TIC structure, which does bear some similarities. I discussed how a Master Lease is utilized for multi-tenant properties and why lenders prefer the DST structure over the former TIC structure. Finally, I described how the new Reg A+ securities laws may transform and greatly expand the market for DSTs. I will now move on to discuss how to find suitable DSTs.

CHAPTER

4

SOURCING DELAWARE STATUTORY TRUSTS

Introduction

Although Delaware Statutory Trusts (DSTs) are a form of real estate, they are classified as a security by the government and can only be obtained through approved distribution channels from properly licensed and qualified individuals. Traditional real estate brokers and agents generally lack the additional licenses and qualifications to offer DSTs to their clients. Therefore, interested investors need to seek out licensed securities representatives to assist them in finding suitable DSTs.

Before discussing how to best locate and qualify an appropriate securities representative, let's first take a moment to better understand the process that an individual must complete and be subject to before he or she can offer DSTs to interested parties.

The first step in becoming a securities representative is to affiliate with a licensed broker-dealer who offers DSTs. This process requires the completion of a detailed questionnaire and background check that includes fingerprinting and verification of relevant prior history by third parties. While any person can apply, there are several statutory disqualifications that would prevent a person from becoming a securities representative, including the following:

- Willfully made or caused to make material misstatements or omitted material facts in applications or reports made to industry organizations

- Previously violated federal securities laws

- Failure to supervise another person who violated securities laws

- Any felony or misdemeanor convictions involving a securities transaction, or making of a false report, bribery, perjury, burglary, or the misappropriation of funds or other listed offenses for a period of ten years from the date of conviction

- Association with any person who is known, or in the exercise of reasonable care should be known, as a person who has been expelled or suspended from the securities industry or found to have caused someone else to be suspended or expelled from the industry

Once an applicant has been properly screened and qualified, they then must study and obtain appropriate securities licenses to be allowed to offer DSTs. The basic license required in most states to offer DSTs is a Series 63 license.[28]

The securities industry is primarily regulated by the Financial Industry Regulatory Authority (FINRA).

> *"A top priority of FINRA is to advance investor confidence in the securities markets through vigorous, fair, and effective enforcement of securities laws and rules. FINRA's Enforcement Department investigates potential securities violations and, when warranted,*

---

28 Some states do not require a Series 63 license to sell DSTs.

brings formal disciplinary actions against firms and their associated persons.

FINRA has the authority to fine, suspend, or bar brokers and firms from the industry and works in cooperation with government enforcement agencies that can also impose criminal penalties.

FINRA may initiate investigations from many varied sources, including examination findings, filings made with FINRA, customer complaints, anonymous tips, automated surveillance reports, and referrals from other regulators or other FINRA departments, among others.

In 2014, FINRA brought 1,397 disciplinary actions against registered individuals and firms, and levied $134 million in fines. Thus, FINRA expelled eighteen firms from the securities industry and 705 brokers, as well as barring 481 individuals from associating with FINRA-regulated firms. In addition, FINRA ordered $32.3 million in restitution to harmed investors.

FINRA also mandates ongoing compliance by securities representatives and will engage in field audits to ensure that all members are in strict compliance with all pertinent regulations."[29]

Since the great recession of 2008, which revealed investor losses that were in many cases the result of poor or inadequate regulation of the securities industry, FINRA has significantly raised compliance and educational standards to improve investor confidence.

---

29 http://www.finra.org/industry/enforcement

Furthermore, many of the securities brokerage firms that offer DSTs also have implemented additional measures to ensure that their representatives can provide clients with a high level of support, including:

- Mandating that their securities representatives study all DSTs offered by their firm and complete a test of their knowledge and understanding of each offering prior to presenting it to their clients

- Completion of annual continuing education programs to ensure that each representative remains abreast of current regulatory requirements

- Annual branch office visits to audit records and procedures for ensuring client confidentiality and proper handling of funds.

In summary, the overall requirements to be able to offer DSTs to clients are considerably more involved than those for becoming a real estate agent. All the additional requirements and enforcement mechanisms still do not fully guarantee that each securities representative will always perform to the expectations of their clients. Let's review some of the ways in which you can determine which representative may best meet your needs.

How to Qualify DST Securities Representatives

Due to time constraints of completing a successful 1031 Exchange, there is often limited time to develop a close relationship with a securities representative who can present DST options to you. Here are several guidelines that you should consider when selecting a DST representative:

Prior Commercial Real Estate Experience Is a Must

Most securities representatives work with stocks, bonds, mutual funds, etc., and do not possess deep knowledge of income-producing real estate offerings. While they may be effective in repeating sound bites from a DST marketing brochure, representatives who lack sufficient real estate background will not be able to answer tough questions on how various DST offerings compare to each other or evaluate projections and other claims of future performance.

When asking qualifying questions of representatives regarding their real estate background, do not make the mistake of thinking that any prior real estate experience is adequate. Seek out representatives with significant experience selling and evaluating income-producing real estate like the asset types in which you plan to invest. If you are leaning toward multifamily properties, ask questions on assessing expenses, net operating income, submarket occupancy rates, etc. Also look into whether they remain active in traditional real estate sales and not just speaking from prior experience that may no longer be relevant.

Obtain and Check References of Recent and Long-Term Clients

An investment in a DST is the start of a long-term relationship with the representative who got you into the deal. Make sure references have a positive story to tell of how committed their representative was to them over the course of prior investments. Questions will be likely to come up over the investment cycle and you will need to be comfortable that your representative will be responsive and won't just disappear after the sale has been made.

Arrange a Face-to-Face Meeting

Make time to meet your representative at their place of business. This will provide an opportunity to get a sense of their organizational skills, their support staff, and their overall success as a business. Representatives who work from home or who have limited support staff are much more likely to come up short when you need them the most. Unexpected things can happen, even with the best investments, and you should feel comfortable that your representative and their firm will be there to support you for the entire investment cycle.

Also note that unless you reside in a major metropolitan area, you may need to interact with a securities representative who is not local to you. This should not automatically be a disqualifier because many investors successfully conclude DST investments with representatives outside of their area. While I am biased toward recommending that clients work with local representatives, it is generally better to work with a more highly qualified representative out of your area than someone local who may lack the needed experience and full credentials to provide comprehensive service to you.

Run a Background Check

In today's internet-enabled world, it is relatively easy to obtain useful background information on licensed professionals. Trade and professional organizations that cater to licensed individuals often have areas on their websites where background checks of their members can be accessed. FINRA provides a site called BrokerCheck (http://brokercheck.finra.org/) that provides information on all currently registered securities brokers and firms.

After putting the name of your prospective representative into the FINRA search screen, you will receive a detailed report that includes employment history, professional qualifications, disciplinary actions, criminal convictions, civil judgments, and arbitration awards. Similar information is also available for the employing brokerage firm, including any pending actions or litigation. Active brokers are required to update information on BrokerCheck with any new information within 30 days.

If your securities representative also possesses a real estate license (which I recommend), you can also go to the Department of Real Estate website in the state where their license is held and receive information similar to that provided by FINRA but pertaining to the representative's activities and history as a real estate professional. Both checks can be completed in just a few minutes and are highly recommended.

Sourcing DSTs

Now that you are armed with information on how to evaluate securities representatives and their firms, you are ready to seek out DSTs. The most common way is to begin an internet search including key words and phrases, such as DST list, 1031 Exchange, asset class preferences (e.g., multifamily, retail, NNN), preferred states, etc., along with your location.

Most of your hits on these key words will take you to internet sites that will ask for further qualifying information prior to presenting you with a list of current DSTs. While this can be annoying and may seem somewhat intrusive, FINRA requires that registered securities representatives only present lists of current DSTs to qualified potential investors. The chief qualifying criteria are that the potential investor provide basic contact information and confirm that they are an accredited investor.

After completing a short registration form, some firms will have a securities representative contact you for further qualification to determine which DSTs may be most suitable to meet your objectives. Other firms will simply send you a list of what they currently have available and then follow up with you after that.

It is worthwhile to initially interact with at least two or three brokerage firms. While most firms will offer many of the same DSTs, the lists will not be identical because there are smaller DST sponsors who offer DSTs directly to investors, and they may have offerings that have not been approved by all the firms that you contact.[30] Brokerage firms have differing standards as to information that they may initially provide when first presenting a DST to a new client. Often the data that you will first see contains limited information covering just the asset type, location, first-year cash-on-cash returns, and loan-to-value (LTV) ratio.[31]

As you complete your initial searches, you will quickly gain a sense of the firm and the specific securities representative who is interacting with you. If your initial impressions are favorable, be sure to further qualify

---

30 Direct offerings of DSTs on the internet can be made by sponsors using a securities exemption called 506(c). Sponsors who utilize this exemption must take added to steps to verify and document the accreditation status of their investors.

31 The LTV ratio is expressed in a two-decimal number (e.g., .57) and is helpful in determining how closely a DST offering may match your 1031 Exchange proceeds.

your representative and their firm per the criteria that I presented earlier in this chapter.

Offering Materials

As previously mentioned, your first exposure to available DSTs will likely be a list covering very basic descriptive information including asset type, location, first-year cash-on-cash returns, and LTV ratio. If you wish to obtain more information, you should request a full offering package. Each DST offering will typically consist of the following documents:

- Private Placement Memorandum: A 100+-page summary of the offering including risk factors, financing terms, property and market information, financial projections, DST trust agreement, tax opinion, third-party reports, leases, loan documents, and a recent property appraisal.

- Marketing Brochure: Highlights the offerings including projected returns, property and location information and photos, financing summary, and information on the sponsor.

- Subscription Documents: Includes a Purchase Agreement and a Purchaser Questionnaire (10+ pages each).

You can request these materials either in hard copy or in electronic form.

Summary

DSTs are available only through registered and qualified securities representatives. Choose your representatives carefully and be sure to complete background checks to verify experience, employment history, complaints, and their overall working relationship with other clients. After obtaining a list of current offerings, be sure to request full offering materials so you are able to access more detailed information on the offerings, including risk factors, potential future performance, property and submarket information, financing details, and other items that will allow you to make an informed decision on the suitability of the investment for your objectives.

In Chapter 5 I will discuss how to evaluate and compare DST offerings.

CHAPTER

5

EVALUATING DELAWARE STATUTORY TRUSTS

Introduction

I will begin this chapter with two very important assumptions:

1) Using the advice that I provided in Chapter 4, you have qualified and selected an experienced Delaware Statutory Trust (DST) securities representative.

2) You have received offering materials on currently available DSTs and narrowed your focus to a subset that you would like to compare with each other and with other investment options that you may have.

Before I discuss our approach to analyzing DSTs, I would like to summarize our background and biases in weighting various factors that I consider.

As of the publication date of this book, our firm has been involved in managing properties owned by both investors in wholly owned real estate and in fractional interests including Tenant in Common (TIC) investments and DSTs for more than fourteen years. We have directly managed well over one hundred and fifty large properties across the United States and have evaluated several hundred more on behalf of investors. During this period, we have also seen the impact of one of the most severe real estate downturns in modern times and the subsequent recovery.

The 2008 crash affected all real estate classes and stress-tested all real estate management firms. Many sponsors and managers who were ill prepared and insufficiently capitalized to weather the storm went out of business, causing many properties to lose management resources at a time when such resources were sorely needed. I also witnessed how certain asset classes held up much better than others and not only did not decline as much, but were also among the first to rebound as the economy improved.

Most recently I have seen growing interest from our large client base in seeking stable income and yields above 5% along with growing frustration in finding suitable investment properties due to high demand fueled by historically low interest rates. Thus, a growing number of real estate investors are considering real estate investments that are managed by larger third parties who may be more adept at finding desirable properties and obtaining attractive financing so that higher yields can be delivered to their investors.

As a long-time manager of real estate, I understand that there are added costs to having a manager take on responsibilities that could be, in some cases, otherwise done by the investor directly. When beginning our business many years ago, the costs charged by third-party managers appeared higher to us than the value that was apparently being provided. While I have gained an appreciation of the amount of work required to find and successfully manage income-producing real estate and have moderated our views on this subject, I remain skeptical of costs that appear out of line with our experience in managing properties and will place a higher negative weight on DST offerings that do not appear to have fair market management and sponsor fees. Given these points, I will now lay out our perspectives on how to evaluate DSTs.

The Sponsor

Our evaluation of DSTs always begins with a fresh evaluation of the quality and prior history of the sponsor. In a DST, virtually all key property decisions are controlled by the trustee, who is typically an affiliate of the sponsor. The trustee and their staff are empowered to not only control many operational aspects of the property, but they are also responsible for investor reporting and assisting clients on an as-needed basis (e.g., transfer of interests, questions on tax matters, etc.). Any weaknesses can potentially have a significant impact on property performance and investor satisfaction.

In contrast to 2005, which was the peak for investments made in TIC-structured properties and when more than one hundred sponsors were in the market, today there are fewer than thirty qualified sponsors of DST offerings. Why? It is much more difficult to qualify as a DST sponsor today for the following reasons:

-   The DST sponsor and their affiliate is solely on the hook for all loan liabilities. The investors/beneficiaries have no loan liabilities and are not required to qualify. To obtain an attractive loan, the sponsor needs to pass the scrutiny of lenders, who are much more concerned today about avoiding losses than they were prior to the 2008 recession.

-   Securities brokers are now warier of doing business with sponsors who fall short in areas of real estate experience, balance sheet, and demonstrated ability to consistently meet investor expectations. Accompanying the decline of real estate values in the 2008 era, many brokers had to suffer losses due to fines imposed by FINRA as well exposure to investor lawsuits related to poor property management and inability to meet stated investment projections. Liability insurance for brokers dramatically increased, causing a heightened sensitivity to approving deals and sponsors that had not been fully vetted by both the securities dealer and by independent third parties.

-   Added regulations and procedures for ongoing compliance with tightened securities laws by FINRA have resulted in a more conservative approach to evaluating the suitability of investments for clients and effectively raised the bar for both new deals and new sponsors.

Here are the key questions that you or your securities representative must research when looking at DST sponsors:

- How long has the sponsor been in business?
- How many DST offerings have they brought to market?
- How many of their DST offering are currently meeting or exceeding published expectations?
- How many of the fractional interest (TIC and DST) offerings have failed to deliver on their original projections?
- Has the sponsor ever invested additional capital from their own funds to improve performance for their clients?
- What is the net worth of the sponsor and their recent financial performance? How likely are they to remain in business for the life of your planned investment?

The Real Estate

The next area to evaluate after narrowing down those sponsors that you wish to consider is the real estate. In this section, I will discuss asset types, location, and property condition considerations.

Assessing real estate can be complex, and I strongly recommend that you enlist the support of a qualified real estate professional to evaluate not only the information in the sponsor's offering package, but also additional information that can be obtained from other sources (e.g., submarket reports, comparable sales, local demographics, etc.).

I recommend that you begin your assessment of the real estate by determining which asset types are most likely to meet your overall objectives. Once you have narrowed down the most desirable asset classes, you will then be in a better position to further compare available offerings within that asset class. It is much easier to compare similar assets to each other than to compare disparate assets, i.e., apartment to apartment versus an apartment relative to an office building.

Let's continue by discussing the more popular DST assets types.

Single-Tenant Triple Net (NNN)

Properties having single tenants with long-term leases where the tenants are fully responsible for all expenses are very popular DST options. You may recall that the DST structure prohibits adding additional capital or renegotiating leases after the DST is introduced. Single-tenant properties with long-term leases are an ideal fit for this structure.

To qualify for financing, remaining lease terms need to be greater than ten years and are often fifteen years or longer. Because the tenant is responsible for all expenses, including building maintenance, repairs, taxes, and insurance, management oversight costs are minimal and generally limited to periodic site inspections, investor reporting, and occasional lease renewal negotiations. Investors seeking these types of assets are comforted by the predictable income and minimal involvement by the owners in day-to-day management.

There are potential downsides that must be considered, however. Most DSTs have loans that expire in ten years and have a significant prepayment penalty if the loan is paid off before it matures. These loans can be assumed by new owners with modest transfer costs, so the prepayment penalty may not come into play if the new owner is accepted by the lender as a qualified borrower. Due to the ten-year loan term, however, most DSTs have a plan to be sold or refinanced close to when the loan matures.

If a sale of single-tenant property is concluded in the tenth year, the remaining lease term will obviously be less than when the investment was first made. The reduced lease term may impact value, particularly if there is any reason to believe that the tenant will not renew their lease. As a practical matter, lease terms of less than ten years will also limit financing options and potentially raise borrowing costs because lenders will want added security that their new loan on the property will be repaid.

While the risk of the tenants not renewing may be low, especially if they are in a location that remains suitable for them, the risk is never zero. Even a Walgreen's in a strong location may move down the street to occupy a newer building.

The other major consideration is that NNN leases have limitations on both the frequency and magnitude of rent bumps that can be realized. In today's low inflationary climate, leases often provide for rent bumps of 1–2% per year, with adjustments made once every five years or less. Should inflation outpace the allowed rent bumps in the lease, the investor may experience lower than desired market returns.

Multifamily

Multifamily DSTs have emerged as the most popular option for investors for several reasons. All multifamily DSTs are structured under a Master Lease, where the sponsor/trustee is solely responsible for all rental income. While the DST structure does not allow primary leases to be renegotiated, the Internal Revenue Service (IRS) has ruled that a Master Lease can be utilized for properties with multiple leases if the Master Lease holder takes on income responsibilities as if they were the only tenant in the property.

The Master Lease holder can enter sub-leases with tenants, but each month they need to pay rent to the DST investors regardless of whether they have sufficient rent coming in from sub-tenants. With a Master Lease structure, multi-tenant properties then appear similar to single-tenant properties.

Many investors prefer multifamily DSTs for the following reasons:

- Rents can be quickly adjusted to changing market conditions
- Unlike single-tenant properties, there are no issues with a declining primary lease term at time of sale
- Multifamily properties have outperformed other sectors in the recent real estate cycle since the 2008 recession

There are several challenges that need to be considered when reviewing specific multifamily offerings. The first is that the DST structure requires that all offerings be fully capitalized up front. No capital calls can be made on the investors in DSTs. Therefore, estimates need to be made by the sponsor of all likely capital expenses that may be required over the full holding period of the investment, and those funds need to be set aside as property reserves to be available when needed.

Determining all potential future expenditures over a ten-year period is a difficult task at best and requires a great deal of multifamily property expertise—and at least some luck that events will play out as expected. If too much money is set aside, investor returns will be compromised, and if too little is set aside, the property may be unable to meet its obligations, resulting in a potential loss of property value.[32]

The process of assessing the adequacy of property reserves in a specific investment is beyond the scope of this book and best left to competent real estate professionals.

Other Asset Classes

Within the constraints of the DST structure I have seen many other asset classes offered by sponsors ranging from medical, storage, student housing, retail, commercial office, and parking lots, among others. Asset classes outside of single-tenant NNN and multifamily will often yield a higher annual return. However, the adage of *the greater the return, the greater the risk* holds for DSTs as well as for other types of investments.

When sharing lists of available DSTs with our clients, I often see a singular focus on advertised annual returns. Some clients will even look no further than the investment that offers the highest annual return. Clearly this overly simplified approach of evaluating investments can raise the risk level beyond what the investor may be willing to tolerate.

Location

Now that you have shortlisted potential sponsors and selected an asset type, you need to consider the location of the property. A first consideration in narrowing down desirable locations is the relative rate of

---

32 In a worst case scenario, there is an option in most DST agreements where the DST can be converted into an LLC partnership structure to allow a capital call to be made so that additional funds can raised (referred to as a Springing LLC). 1031 Exchanges are not allowed form out of an LLC partnership structure, so the benefit of future tax deferrals would be lost.

population growth. States with leading net population growth are Florida, Texas, North and South Carolina, Arizona, Colorado, and Oregon.

Another consideration is the level of state income taxes where the property is located. States with no income tax include Alaska, Florida, Nevada, South Dakota, Texas, Washington, and Wyoming. The combination of strong net population growth and low or no taxes result in Florida and Texas having the highest concentration of DST investment options.

Digging deeper, you should then evaluate submarket trends within the state to determine the degree to which property values of comparable assets are likely to increase over the holding period. Investors also consider weather hazard probability, i.e., hurricanes, tornadoes, etc., although these location risks are often mitigated by property insurance.

Property Condition

The DST prohibition against investing additional funds for capital improvements after the DST is first formed tends to rule out properties that may require significant repairs or upgrades. While it is common for real estate investors to purchase distressed properties, improve them, and then sell them for tidy profits, DST properties are typically already stabilized at the time of the investment. Although I have seen older properties dating back to 1979 in DST structures, most DSTs are newer, fully leased properties that are earning income at the time of investment.

While some DSTs are described as value-add opportunities and promise higher future returns because of planned improvements, the degree of renovation that takes place is modest, such as new appliances, fresh paint and carpeting, new common area amenities, etc. A description of the property, including planned improvements, environmental conditions, and related restrictions (e.g., zoning, covenants, easements, and other encumbrances) can be found in the Offering Memorandum (OM).

If available, it is useful to review the property appraisal and property condition reports that were prepared to obtain the loan. These reports will describe the property condition in significant detail as well as provide useful information on the current value of the property.

If possible, I also encourage investors to visit properties prior to investing because new information is almost sure to be discovered. In some cases, DST sponsors will reimburse the cost of property visits, so if you are inclined to visit before you invest, be sure ask to your securities representative if travel costs will be covered.

Offering Details

A great deal of useful information can be obtained by reading through the OM. This document is typically over one hundred pages long and will contain a fair amount of legal terms and boilerplate along with sometimes scary risk disclosures, e.g., *all real estate investments are subject to uncontrollable risks and investors may lose their full investment*. It is nevertheless well worth your time to review the OM and jot down questions and concerns that can be discussed with your securities representative or, if needed, with the sponsor directly.

Appendix A in this book contains a typical Table of Contents for a DST OM and provides an overview of what you should expect when you receive one. While individual investors should not expect to be able to negotiate any of the offering terms, it is useful to compare offerings to better understand any unusual or non-market terms that could affect overall investor expectations.

Selling Costs

Most investors will raise questions that boil down to *How can I be sure I am getting a fair deal?* As with all managed investments, there are expenses associated with acquiring, managing, and ultimately disposing of properties that will need to be paid to third parties. Investors should feel comfortable that they are paying fair market rate fees for the services provided.

While the number of sponsors has significantly declined relative to those that were offering TIC properties, competitive forces in the industry have pushed down sales and management costs over the past several years. Almost all categories of selling costs, including commissions, management fees, and mark-ups, are relatively lower today on average compared to past years.

Investors who are new to DST investments should understand that between 8% and 15% of their investment dollars will go to third parties and will not be invested directly into the asset. The asset will then need to appreciate to offset these costs to return the full amount of invested equity plus profits when the property is ultimately sold.

A summary of all selling costs as well as how other funds are planned to be utilized is found in the Estimated Use of Proceeds section in the OM. It is worthwhile to compare the charts that summarize the use of proceeds between the options that you have shortlisted.

Management Costs

The OM will also provide a summary of applicable ongoing management costs including asset and property management fees, leasing commissions, and any additional fees collected by the manager. The trustee will commonly act as an asset manager for the property, overseeing local management functions that may be performed by third parties, as well as taking on a primary role in investor communications and executing the overall strategy for the property.

Back-End Costs

When the property is eventually sold, the trustee will charge a disposition fee for overseeing the sale. This fee will vary depending on whether third-party broker fees are included. I prefer to see the full sale costs disclosed as a fixed not-to-exceed percentage rather than an undetermined market fee.

Loan Details

The loan details will be found in the Financing Terms section. The property loan can be an important differentiator when evaluating DSTs. The first consideration is the loan-to-value (LTV) ratio. If you are doing a 1031 Exchange into a DST (versus a cash investment), the LTV should closely match the LTV of the property that you are selling. Differences in LTV ratio of the sold or relinquished property and the DST LTV can result in tax consequences that may cause you to favor one offering over another.

Another factor to consider is the degree to which the loan contains an interest-only component. Many DST loans have an initial interest-only period that is followed by increased debt service payments that include an amortization component that pays down loan principal. Many (but not all) investors favor loans with longer interest-only periods because monthly cashflow is maximized when no principal payments are required.

The Financing Terms section will also detail the amount of required reserves mandated by the lender. Some sponsors may want added reserves beyond what the lender requires and, if so, you will find that information in the OM discussing the planned use of all such reserves.

Finally, you will find a summary of loan guarantees required by the lender. Loans for DSTs are characterized as non-recourse loans, although there are situations that may arise where the lender can claim funds from the guarantor, known as bad boy carve-outs. While it is very rare that guarantees are triggered, it is worth reviewing this section and jotting down questions to ask your securities representative on any areas that raise concerns or you do not fully understand. Keep in mind that investors in a DST do not have any loan responsibilities and therefore would not be subject to any loan recourse.

Exit Strategy

The exit strategy for the property will be presented in the Business Plan section and should be reviewed and compared against your other short-listed options. The most common exit strategy is to sell the property seven to ten years after it was first structured as a DST. This timeframe is required for the property to appreciate sufficiently to cover the initial selling costs and return your original investment plus a projected profit.

Due to prepayment penalties that are likely to exist on DST loans, sales that take place significantly before the loan maturity date (typically ten years from the original offering date) would most likely be done by having the buyer assume the loan. A loan assumption would not be subject to a prepayment penalty; however, a loan transfer fee—typically 1%—plus other miscellaneous costs would need to be paid.

If your DST investment consists of multiple properties, there are several additional areas that you need to evaluate. Portfolios appeal to investors who seek diversification benefits with multiple properties in a single investment. While it is relatively easy to diversify DST investments due to low minimums ($25,000 or less), each separate property has some associated overhead in terms of managing paperwork, filing taxes, etc. Having a diversified portfolio of properties in a single investment can streamline investment management—much like investing in a mutual fund rather than in separate stocks.

The first area to understand is whether the portfolio of properties is encumbered under a single loan. If so, it is likely that all the properties are pledged as security for the loan and would need to be sold as a group to a subsequent buyer. Multiple properties in a single offering are often cross-collateralized and cannot be broken up and sold individually. I am wary of cross-collateralized DST offerings because it adds uncertainty as to whether a future buyer will have an interest in buying all properties or only buying some. If a buyer determines that some of the properties in a portfolio are less attractive or less of a fit for their investment strategy, they will discount the price that they are willing to offer for the entire portfolio.

Currently there are several sponsors offering portfolios where the stated exit strategy is to sell the portfolio to a larger investment firm such as a real estate investment trust. There is often an assumption in these strategies that real estate investment trusts may pay a premium for a stabilized portfolio due to economies of scale in acquiring multiple properties in a single transaction. If you are considering a DST offering where the exit strategy is to sell the entire portfolio to a larger financial firm, I encourage you to request comparable examples of such transactions to gain confidence that the sponsor will be able to execute this type of strategy.

I prefer DST portfolios that allow the sponsor/trustee to sell each property individually when market conditions are optimum. Even this scenario can have its issues, however, because a partial sale of a full portfolio would generate less proceeds than would be available for a subsequent 1031 Exchange. This would also be the case in splitting investment funds among multiple individual investments.

Summary

In this chapter, I have outlined a process for evaluating and comparing DSTs. I have stressed the critical importance of first qualifying sponsors on the basis of their track record of producing investor returns and then seeking out a qualified securities representative with commercial real estate experience to help you better assess various offerings. While multifamily assets appear to be in the greatest demand in the current real estate cycle, other asset classes can also provide suitable investment opportunities subject to the trade-offs that I outlined.

6

DELAWARE STATUTORY TRUST SPONSORS

Introduction

In this chapter, I will provide an overview of the major active sponsors who provide Delaware Statutory Trust (DST) offerings.

The number of firms offering fractional real estate interests peaked in 2006 and then declined dramatically during the 2008 recession, which forced many of the less capitalized firms to close. As DSTs rose in popularity in recent years, increased scrutiny by lenders and broker-dealers has limited the entry of new sponsors, as all new sponsors are required to meet increasingly strenuous standards. Today there are fewer than thirty sponsors of fractional real estate products, including DSTs and Tenant in Common (TICs), as compared to over one hundred in 2006. Before discussing individual sponsors, let's cover some general background on DST sponsors and how they differ from other types of real estate investment firms.

Role of a DST Sponsor

A DST sponsor has much in common with other firms who locate and manage investment real estate on behalf of investors:

- They work closely with the real estate brokerage community to find attractively priced offerings that are suitable for investors, typically off-market properties that are not being publicly marketed.

- They have close relationships with multiple loan providers who can provide optimum financing to allow investors to reap maximum income from their investments.

- They tend to specialize in asset classes and geographies.

- They possess sufficient infrastructure to maintain ongoing investor and lender reporting.

DST sponsors are differentiated from traditional real estate investment managers in the following ways:

- They are responsible for obtaining loans, are solely responsible to the lender for any loan guarantees, and must meet balance sheet requirements to support multiple loans.

- They typically take ownership of their properties prior to exposing them to investors, thereby taking on added capital risk, if their offerings are not fully subscribed, they are left with any unsold interests, and their capital is tied up until the asset is sold.

- Their offerings are sold through licensed securities brokers, who impose added levels of due diligence and ongoing performance scrutiny.

- Their offerings are approved for sale to investors subject to third-party due diligence reports that summarize offering structure, fees, and prior performance of the sponsor, among other items.

Due primarily to the requirement of capital risk and heightened scrutiny by the broker-dealer community, relatively few real estate management firms participate in sponsoring DST offerings.

Let's now move on to the profiles of the major industry participants. The data given below are believed to be current as of the publication date of this book. So as to not raise questions regarding any biases, we are listing the sponsors in alphabetical order. As you review these summaries, keep in mind *that past performance is not a guarantee of future success*.

AEI (www.aeifunds.com)

Founded in 1970, AEI is one of the country's oldest sponsors of net leased real estate investment programs, as well as a leader in the 1031 property exchange industry. The firm has been completing successful fractional 1031 exchanges on behalf of investors since 1992. As a pioneer in this business, AEI was the first sponsor to receive a favorable private letter ruling with regards to its offering structure in 2003.

AEI DSTs offer quality, single-tenant, freestanding properties occupied by corporate tenants under long-term net leases. All of this is done debt-free, without the use of any leverage or mortgage financing, which reduces investment, refinancing, and foreclosure risk. AEI offerings provide for passive real estate ownership of commercial properties with the goal of stable income, low volatility, reduced risk, and capital appreciation.

To date, AEI has offered one hundred and thirty net lease investment programs to more than twenty thousand investors nationwide. Of these offerings, ninety-five have been 1031-focused and seven have been structured as DSTs. No DSTs have yet gone full cycle. The firm has purchased more than 390 properties in forty-one states with a combined value of more than $1 billion. AEI utilizes the 506(b) exemption for their sponsored offerings.

Bluerock (www.bluerockre.com)

Bluerock is a private equity real estate investment firm founded in 2010 and based in New York, NY. They are a full-service, national investment firm offering a mix of public and private institutional investments, with both short- and long-term goals, to real estate investors. Bluerock's senior management team has an average of over twenty-five years investing experience and has acquired or developed more than eighty-five real estate properties. This includes forty-eight apartment properties with more than ten thousand apartment units, representing approximately fourteen million combined square feet across fourteen states and more than $2 billion in acquisition value.

They currently have more than $2.3 billion of real estate assets under management, with the majority being apartment communities in sought-after growth areas throughout the United States. Bluerock leverages strong relationships with regional partners, including many of the nation's largest apartment developers and managers, to bring local knowledge and experience to their projects.

One main differentiator for the sponsor is their involvement in ground-up construction of apartment complexes across the country, and they currently have more than two thousand new apartment units under development. In addition, Bluerock seeks stabilized, income-generating properties as well as value-add investments, creating a diverse footprint across the most desirable real estate markets in the country. While relatively new to the DST marketplace, Bluerock has demonstrated their ability to provide a return on investment and therefore have attracted more than ten thousand real estate investors to their offerings nationwide.

Cantor Fitzgerald (www.cantor.com)

One of the newest sponsors to enter the DST market, Cantor Fitzgerald is also one of the oldest companies to be participating in the space. Founded in 1945 in New York, NY, Cantor Fitzgerald has established itself as one of the dominant global financial service firms with significant real estate, capital markets, research, and investment expertise. The company has a significant presence across the world, with more than ten thousand employees in over one hundred and fifty offices across twenty-two countries. As a company, they conduct more than $180 trillion of financial transactions annually and have recently invested more than $600 million to establish a multi-disciplined real estate platform with capabilities spanning the investment cycle, including acquisitions, financing, property management, leasing, and investment sales. Boasting an investment-grade credit rating by both Standard & Poor's and Fitch Ratings, they are well positioned to become a dominant force in the DST marketplace.

Since entering the DST sector, Cantor Fitzgerald has made five DST programs available to investors, none of which have gone full cycle.[33] While their long-term asset strategy is to offer a diversified platform to meet different investors' needs, up until now, they have solely focused on triple net retail offerings. Cantor differs from other sponsors in terms of their overall size and scale as a company as well as being the only investment-grade sponsor in the DST marketplace. Their entry into the DST market underscores the growing interest of this area to institutional real estate firms. Their programs currently utilize the 506(b) exemption structure.

Capital Square 1031 (www.capitalsquare1031.com)

Capital Square 1031 is a national real estate investment and management company that sponsors institutional-quality real estate exchange programs that qualify for tax deferral under Section 1031 of the Internal Revenue Code. The firm uses the DST structure to make quality real estate investments available to a larger number of investors.

Capital Square 1031 was founded in 2012 and has sponsored thirty-five DST programs to date. None of the DST programs have gone full cycle; most have a seven-to-ten-year holding period, and the oldest programs are approaching the mid-point of their holding period. While the firm is primarily focused on DST programs, a new REIT is being launched near the publication date of this book to capitalize on value-add medical office properties.

Capital Square 1031 focuses on acquiring stable multifamily apartment communities and long-term triple net leased medical properties across the nation. The apartment communities are in well-established neighborhoods surrounded by centers of employment and numerous recreational opportunities. The medical properties are leased by

---

33 *Full cycle* refers to the full investment timeline including initial investment, ongoing management, and eventual sale of the property with all investor returns being realized by the investor.

investment-grade tenants on a triple net, long-term basis with regular rental increases, making for a predictable and increasing income stream in a recession-resistant investment where the tenant pays virtually all operating expenses. The goal is to provide investors predictable cash-flow and the potential for capital appreciation from stable replacement properties that qualify for tax deferral under Section 1031.

Capital Square 1031 provides a range of services, including acquisition, due diligence, loan sourcing, property management/asset manage-ment, and disposition, for a growing number of high net worth investors, private equity firms, family offices, and institutional investors across the nation. The firm oversees a growing national portfolio of fifty-four real estate assets valued at over $541 million (based on investment cost). In September 2016, the firm was ranked as the second fastest growing company in the Richmond, VA, area by Richmond BizSense, with 274% annual revenue growth from 2013 to 2015.

ExchangeRight (www.exchangeright.com)

ExchangeRight is based in Pasadena, CA, and initiated their syndication of 1031 DST offerings in 2012. The firm currently has more than 3.2 million square feet of assets under man-agement, valued at approximately $550 million. Their 195+ properties are located throughout twenty-seven states and are structured to provide long-term, stable income and asset preservation for accredited 1031 investors.

Until recently, ExchangeRight has exclusively focused on net leased retail assets with investment-grade corporate tenants who operate in the necessity retail space (e.g., Walgreens). In 2015, they began a new multifamily platform focused on Class B apartments with stable income and value-added upside potential. Their multifamily program is described as featuring strong cashflow, high debt-coverage ratios, con-servative underwriting, long-term fixed-rate financing, and the potential to enhance return with value-added strategies.

To date, ExchangRight has offered fourteen DST programs and none have yet gone full cycle. They report that their actual returns have met their average projected returns of 7.3%. While relatively new to the DST market place, the introduction of a multifamily platform is expected to broaden their appeal to potential DST investors. Their programs currently utilize the 506(b) exemption structure.

Four Springs Capital Trust (www.fsctrust.com)

Four Springs Capital Trust is a multifaceted real estate company that was founded in 2012 and is based in Lake Como, NJ. The firm offers both real estate investment trusts (REITs) and DST investments focused on net-leased single-tenant retail, medical office, and industrial/warehouse assets. Four Springs targets triple net and double net leased properties that have lease terms greater than ten years and investment-grade tenants. They will, however, consider private companies with strong balance sheets and income history.

With a national footprint, Four Springs separates itself from other sponsors by pursuing build-to-suit properties that are acquired directly from developers. Four Springs' goal is to mitigate risk from economic downturns in local markets by diversifying their DST offerings. They seek to accomplish this by acquiring a greater amount of small single-tenant properties as opposed to a small amount of large multi-tenant properties.

To date, Four Springs has fully funded five DST offerings, with none of them having gone full cycle. Four Springs' key differentiators include its policy to co-invest in every offering and to not charge a disposition fee on the sale of the property. Additionally, investors are offered the opportunity to trade their DST interests for interests in a Four Springs REIT by way of a tax-deferred exchange. This allows the avoidance of transaction costs on the back end. Their programs currently utilize the 506(b) exemption structure.

Inland Real Estate Investment Corporation (www.inlandgroup.com)

Inland Real Estate Investment Corporation was originally founded in 1969 in Oak Brook, IL. Inland has sponsored over 704 programs across forty-three states, including seven REITs, 687 private placement offerings, and ten limited partnerships. With over $10.5 billion of completed transactions and more than 490,000 investors, Inland is one of the most experienced sponsors in the market engaging in all facets of real estate, including property management, leasing, marketing, acquisition, disposition, development, redevelopment, renovation, construction, and finance.

The Inland Real Estate Group of Companies is a fully-integrated group of legally and financially independent companies, with Inland Private Capital Corporation being the specific arm of the company that sponsors 1031 DST properties. The Inland Private Capital Corporation was formed in 2001, and as of September 2015 it has offered more than $2.394 billion in equity investments to over 7,080 investors. Of the properties that they have sponsored, 353 are retail centers, forty-eight are office buildings, nine are industrial and distribution centers, and twenty-six are multifamily communities. Of these properties, 64% were existing construction while 36% were new construction, and as of September 4, 2015, sixty of the assets have been sold.

One of Inland's strengths is their alignment with investors through direct investments of $113 million into their own programs. Not only are they one of the most dominant DST sponsors in the market, but as demonstrated by the above figures, Inland is considered one of the largest investment, commercial real estate, and financial institutions in the country.

Moody (www.moodynational.com) Hotels/Hosp

Moody National Realty is the subsidiary of Moody National Companies that acquires and syndicates real estate offerings across the United States. They are an all-encompassing real estate company operating subsidiary companies focused on mortgage lending, development, management, syndication, title, and insurance. Moody National Companies was formed in 1996, and it is headquartered in Houston, TX.

Moody National Realty has been involved in the acquisition and syndication of real estate since its inception, with a total of forty-six privately offered real estate programs funded by more than 1,250 investors, producing a total capitalization of approximately $1.4 billion. In addition,

Moody National Realty specializes in hospitality assets throughout the United States and has acquired more than sixty-five class A hotel properties.

Although Moody has sponsored many various real estate investment offerings, only recently have they begun syndicating real estate in the DST structure, with a total of two DST offerings having been fully funded to date. Neither has gone full cycle.

Moody National Realty's primary focus for their DST platform is the syndication of triple net retail and multifamily properties. They target well-maintained class A assets that are located along the East and West Coasts as well as in the Sun Belt region. Their investment criteria include a focus on major metropolitan population centers located in states that are ranked within the top quartile of U.S. population growth. Additional attributes include an expanding local employment base, a major university, as well as assets with stable and sustainable cashflow in place at the time of acquisition. Moody's programs currently utilize the 506(b) exemption structure.

High LTV

No to Low Income   Higher Risk

Net Lease Capital Advisors (www.netleasecapital.com)

Net Lease Capital Advisors was formed in 1996 and is based in Nashua, NH. Since their inception, they have closed over $9 billion worth of real estate transactions. Net Lease Capital Advisors focuses exclusively on single-tenant triple net properties and has predominantly syndicated highly levered, zero cashflow DST offerings.[34] The properties they pursue tend to be larger in scale with credit tenants rated BBB- or better, including government tenants and national company headquarters.

Their acquisition criteria include preferred lease terms in the 15–20+-year range with transaction sizes ranging anywhere from $20 million to more than $500 million. One of the more experienced DST sponsors, Net Lease Capital Advisor's platform primarily addresses the niche market of those investors looking for high-debt investments with little

---

34 Zero cashflow properties have very high loan-to-value (LTV) ratios (80% and higher) and are attractive to 1031 Exchange investors who are selling properties with high LTVs. High-LTV properties could result from loss of equity due to

to no income due to the objective of avoiding taxes.Net Lease Capital Advisors has fully funded nine DST offerings to date, with one of them having gone full cycle. Their first completed program was the Sun Microsystems Headquarters property, which they re-tenanted upon lease expiration and refinanced the debt to create a positive return for investors. Facebook's corporate headquarters are currently in this building, which is located East Palo Alto, CA. Net Lease Capital Advisors currently utilizes the 506(b) exemption structure.

Passco (www.passco.com) Multi-Family

Passco Companies was founded in 1998 and is headquartered in Irvine, CA. Passco is a nationally recognized real estate investment firm that specializes in the acquisition, development, and management of multifamily and commercial properties throughout the United States. With assets spanning twenty states, they have surpassed $3 billion in acquisitions and are approaching $2 billion of assets under management. They have more than five thousand investors worldwide.

The Passco management team averages thirty-four years of real estate experience and has collectively acquired more than $30 billion of investment real estate projects across the country. Passco seeks to acquire primarily core and value-add multifamily properties with 200+ units as well as retail properties and regional shopping centers in California, Washington, Arizona, Nevada, and Texas. In recent years, Passco has focused exclusively on multifamily properties for their DST offerings.

Passco is one of the most active and successful companies in the DST space. They have acquired and fully funded twenty-seven DST offerings, with one of them having completed the investment cycle. Passco projects returns for their investment offerings in the range of 8–10%, but they produced actual returns of 12–13% on their first full-cycle DST program. Passco represents their key differentiator to be their consistently conservative underwriting, which allows them to exceed their projections and

---

poorly performing real estate; however, owed taxes may still be significant due to recapture of depreciation benefits.

withstand the ebb and flow of real estate cycles. They currently utilize the 506(b) exemption structure.

Provasi (www.provasicapital.com)

Provasi Capital Partners is based in Addison, TX, and was launched from a predecessor platform in October 2015. Provasi provides investment options from multiple managers/sponsors. Their mission is to help financial advisors and their clients preserve wealth through access to unique options for allocating capital, managing risk, and diversifying assets. They also provide market insights, education, and business development solutions to help financial advisors create more meaningful relationships with their clients.

Provasi has offered six DST programs, which were all sponsored by Behringer-Harvard, a thirty-year-old real estate investment firm also based in Addison, TX.

Real Estate Value Advisors, LLC (www.revacompanies.com)

Office

Based in Richmond, VA, Real Estate Value Advisors, LLC (REVA) was formed in 2005 by a team of seasoned real estate professionals with more than fifty years of experience and $12 billion in transactions, including twelve DSTs. With more than a decade of history and nearly $400 million in sponsored transactions, REVA is one of the few sponsors of fractional real estate offerings to weather the 2008 storm and expand its offerings.

Relative to other DST sponsors, REVA predominantly focuses on office properties. In addition to syndications for 1031 Exchange and cash investors in the DST structure, REVA also sponsors the REVA Catalyst Fund, which acquires office properties with value-add characteristics where there is a need for capital infusion, repositioning, or refinancing.

Summary

In this chapter I profiled the better-known current DST sponsors. Firms that were not included should not automatically be disqualified because there are, and will be, many other experienced firms that will gain visibility as the DST marketplace continues to grow. Be sure to review the sponsor websites for any DST offerings you seek out as new and additional information found there may help you further assess the suitability of their offerings in meeting your personal objectives.

CHAPTER

7

THE ROAD AHEAD

First, thanks very much for reading this book. I hope that the information contained herein will assist you in refining investment options that will help you better achieve your financial goals.

The Delaware Statutory Trust (DST) has gained popularity primarily due to rulings by the Internal Revenue Service that allow the structure to be used for tax-deferred 1031 Exchanges. While the 1031 Exchange has been in existence since 1921, it must be emphasized that tax laws are the creation of government entities and that what the government allows one day can be changed the next.

It is estimated that in calendar year 2011 alone, over $30 billion in gains were deferred by taxpayers.[35] This has not gone unnoticed in Washington. As of the publication date of this book, there have been a growing number of politicians from both major parties calling for tax reform as a solution for improving the economy while reducing the very large debt burden that we face today. Many in Washington believe that it is time to update 1031 Exchange rules and reduce the benefits that it provides, especially to more affluent taxpayers. Right or wrong, the 1031 Exchange is now in the spotlight as a *loophole* and is viewed by many politicians to be a vehicle for tax avoidance by the wealthy. Recent developments supporting this point of view include the following:

35https://www.world-finance-conference.com/papers_wfc2/727.pdf

- In 2013, the Senate Finance Committee issued a Tax Reform Discussion Draft that contained proposals ranging from reducing the scope of 1031 Exchanges to the outright repeal of the entire code section.

- The House Ways and Means Committee proposed a total repeal of Section 1031 in 2014.

- The White House, in its 2016 budget, proposed limiting 1031 Exchanges to $1 million per taxpayer per year, which presumably would push the benefit of a 1031 Exchange down to the middle class.

- In June 2016, Speaker of the House Paul Ryan and House Ways and Means Committee Chairman Kevin Brady released a tax reform framework that included provisions to reduce the attractiveness of 1031 Exchanges by replacing existing depreciation deductions with a full deductibility of expenses for commercial properties at the time of investment.

- Fortunately, those proposals have not gone forward, but many of people associated with these committees remain influential in Washington. It is safe to assume that whenever Congress convenes to discuss budgets, tax reform will be a serious topic—and it's hard not to believe that modifications of the 1031 Exchange won't be part of the discussion. Section 1031 has proven to be a very valuable tool for real estate owners and developers.

Critics of efforts to curtail tax-deferred exchanges point out that Congress has made several erroneous assumptions. The first is an assumption that weakening the ability of taxpayers to defer taxes will result in large tax payments to the government that will be available to fund new programs and pay down the debt. I, however, know from our many discussions with real estate investors that they would be less likely to sell their income properties if they had to pay a large tax bill.

Second, proponents of these changes believe that only wealthy taxpayers take advantage of exchanges. Our experience with thousands of investors indicates that for every investor who is reinvesting more than $1 million in gains, there are easily ten other investors who are doing exchanges for less than $1 million. Furthermore, many of our 1031 Exchange investors are older and engaging in exchanges to bolster meager retirement income as well as for estate planning purposes so that their heirs may have a better life.

Third, assumptions of how additional money will flow to the government if exchanges are compromised are wildly overstated. The amount of revenue that politicians think they will collect if exchanges are abolished (and if everyone will continue to sell their investment real estate) is dramatically greater than what occurred even at the top of the real estate market in 2006 and 2007.

Real estate investors generally hold for long-term appreciation and do not rush into panic sales when government policies change. Through experience they know that, as Will Rogers once stated, "They ain't making it anymore" and that real estate values consistently increase over time.

In 2015, a consortium of real estate-related trade associations commissioned the accounting firm of Ernst & Young to analyze the economic impact of repealing like-kind exchanges. Their initial findings, which were further updated in 2016, concluded that repealing the like-kind exchange rules would reduce gross domestic product (GDP), slow economic growth, and negatively impact owners of real property and many U.S. businesses. The most recent data as of 2016 indicate that the ten most affected industries, including real estate, construction, truck transportation, and equipment/vehicle rental and leasing, would suffer an annual year-after-year decline in GDP of $27.5 billion, up from $26 billion in the original report.[36]

Per Margo McDonnell, a recent president of the Federation of Exchange Accommodators, "The conclusions of this study underscore how critical

---

36 http://www.1031taxreform.com/1031press-release/#PR-revised

like-kind exchanges are to the U.S. economy. Small and mid-sized businesses, farmers, ranchers, real estate investors, farm and heavy equipment lessors, trucking companies, and conservation associations are among the broad spectrum of Americans that benefit from like-kind exchanges to invest in their businesses, their communities, their local economies, and in healthy green spaces for the enjoyment of the public and wildlife."

In 2015, Dr. David Ling, finance professor at the University of Florida's Warrington College of Business, and Dr. Milena Petrova, finance professor at Syracuse University's Whitman School of Management, published a study based on their analysis of more than 1.6 million real estate transactions totaling $4.6 trillion over an eighteen-year period (1997–2014).[37] Key findings included:

Like-kind exchanges encourage investment. On average, taxpayers using a like-kind exchange acquire replacement property that is $305,000–$422,000 more valuable than the relinquished property, while replacement properties not using an exchange are of lower or equal value.

Like-kind exchanges contribute significant federal tax revenue. In 34% of exchanges, some federal tax is paid in the year of the exchange. More importantly, over the long run, like-kind exchanges boost tax revenue because of the higher tax liability that arises in the years following the initial exchange.

Like-kind exchanges lead to job creation. Real estate acquired through a like-kind exchange is associated with greater investment and capital expenditures (i.e., job-creating property upgrades and improvements) than real estate acquired without the use of like-kind exchange.

Like-kind exchanges result in less debt. When the price of the replacement property is close to or less than the price of the relinquished property, like-kind exchanges result in a 10% reduction in borrowing, or leverage, at the time of the acquisition.

Per their study, if like-kind exchange rules are repealed:

---

37 http://www.1031taxreform.com/ling-petrova-authors/

Taxes would increase for thousands of commercial property owners. For a typical property owner who defers his or her gain on a commercial property, repealing like-kind exchanges would raise the effective tax rate on the taxpayer's investment (including rental income and gain, based on a nine-year holding period) from 23% to 30%.

Property values would drop. For a commercial property to generate the same rate of return for the investor (if Section 1031 were repealed), prices would have to decline. In local markets and states with moderate levels of taxation, commercial property price would have to decline 8–12% to maintain required equity returns for investors expecting to use like-kind exchanges when disposing of properties. These price declines would reduce the wealth of a large cross-section of households and slow or stop construction in many local markets.

Rents would increase. Over time, real rents would need to increase 8–13% before new construction would become economically viable. These higher rents would reduce the affordability of commercial space for both large and small tenants. Furthermore, the price declines and rent effects of eliminating real estate like-kind exchanges would be more pronounced in high-tax states.

Real estate sales activity would decline. Like-kind exchanges increase the liquidity of the real estate market. An analysis of 336,572 properties that were acquired and sold between 1997 and 2014 showed that properties have significantly shorter holding periods.[38]

The authors conclude their study with the following summary:

> *"Like-kind exchanges are associated with increased investment, shorter holding periods, and lower leverage ... the removal of exchanges will lead to a decrease in investment, an increase in holding periods (decrease in liquidity), and an increase in the use of leverage to finance acquisitions. These micro effects are likely to have macro-economic consequences as*

---

38 http://eyeonhousing.org/2015/07/
new-study-highlights-importance-of-like-kind-exchange-rules/

*well. For example, decreased construction and invest-
ment activity in commercial real estate markets will
depress employment in sectors and markets where
like-kind exchanges are commonly used."*

Steps to Preserve the 1031 Exchange

Since the proposals to repeal or limit Section 1031 appeared, a growing number of regional, state, and local business associations have formally registered their support for like-kind exchanges and called on Congress to preserve this vital economic stimulus. Actions underway include meetings with Congress and ongoing letter writing.

In a May 10, 2016, letter, members of the Section 1031 Like-Kind Exchange Coalition advocated Senate Finance Committee leaders to retain like-kind exchanges to grow the economy, create jobs, and raise wages. Like-kind exchanges are *integral to the efficient operation and ongoing vitality* of thousands of American businesses that contribute to the U.S. economy and job creation. Signers stated that like-kind exchanges promote uniformly agreed upon tax reform goals such as economic growth, job creation, and increased competitiveness. A copy of this letter is found in Appendix C.

If you would like to lend your voice to efforts directed at preserving Section 1031 as a part of the tax code and an important tool in your personal investment planning techniques, what can you do? The Federation of Exchange Accommodators (http://www.1031taxreform.com) has created an excellent resource that can assist interested parties in expressing their concerns over potential changes in the tax code. As a first step, go to their website and become more familiar with information supporting the 1031 Exchange. This website includes a section entitled "Join the Campaign," which provides several useful tools that you can use to express concerns and be heard.

Personal letters (not form letters) written to your Congressional representatives can be very helpful. Better yet, simply call the offices of your Congressional representatives with a prepared script of talking points. While you are unlikely to speak directly with your representative, you will have an opportunity to talk with an aide, who will be obligated to take notes, ask questions, and hopefully follow through with his or her boss. This approach will have the best probability of having your concerns at least noted rather going into a trash can.

Summary

There is much evidence that like-kind exchanges promote efficient expansion of U.S. businesses while stimulating overall economic growth. Exchanges are used not only by individual investors but also by farmers, ranchers, recreational landowners, equipment and machinery owners, and many other businesses that invest in real estate and other capital assets.

While like-kind exchange tax benefits have been in existence since the early part of the last century, there can be no certainty that future benefits will remain intact. All stakeholders who benefit from exchanges are encouraged to contact their Congressional representatives to push for preservation of Section 1031.

I close by wishing all readers the best of success in your future investment endeavors, and I hope that at least some of our readers will be motivated to support efforts to preserve tax-deferred exchanges.

APPENDIX

OFFERING MEMORANDUM TABLE OF CONTENTS EXAMPLE

OFFERING MEMORANDUM EXAMPLE

TABLE OF CONTENTS

APPENDIX A / Offering Memorandum Table of Contents Example

EXHIBITS:

A   Purchaser Questionnaire
B   Purchase Agreement
C   Trust Agreement
D   Projections of Operations for the Project and Return to the Holders
E   Tax Opinion
F   CD with Third Party Reports for the Projects, the Leases and
    Loan Documents

B

IRS REVENUE RULING 2004-86

Internal Revenue Bulletin: 2004-33

August 16, 2004

Revenue Ruling 2004-86

Classification of Delaware statutory trust. This ruling explains how a Delaware statutory trust described in the ruling will be classified for federal tax purposes and whether a taxpayer may acquire an interest in the Delaware statutory trust without recognition of gain or loss under section 1031 of the Code. Rev. Ruls. 78-371 and 92-105 distinguished.

ISSUE(S)

(1) In the situation described below, how is a Delaware statutory trust, described in Del. Code Ann. title 12, §§ 3801 - 3824, classified for federal tax purposes?

(2) In the situation described below, may a taxpayer exchange real property for an interest in a Delaware statutory trust without recognition of gain or loss under § 1031 of the Internal Revenue Code?

FACTS

On January 1, 2005, *A*, an individual, borrows money from *BK*, a bank, and signs a 10-year note bearing adequate stated interest, within the meaning of § 483.On January 1, 2005, *A* uses the proceeds of the loan to purchase Blackacre, rental real property. The note is secured by Blackacre and is nonrecourse to *A*.

Immediately following *A*'s purchase of Blackacre, *A* enters into a net lease with *Z* for a term of 10 years. Under the terms of the lease, *Z* is to pay all taxes, assessments, fees, or other charges imposed on Blackacre by federal, state, or local authorities. In addition, *Z* is to pay all insurance, maintenance, ordinary repairs, and utilities relating to Blackacre. *Z* may sublease Blackacre. *Z*'s rent is a fixed amount that may be adjusted by a formula described in the lease agreement that is based upon a fixed rate or an objective index, such as an escalator clause based upon the Consumer Price Index, but adjustments to the rate or index are not within the control of any of the parties to the lease. Z's rent is not contingent on Z's ability to lease the property or on Z's gross sales or net profits derived from the property.

Also on January 1, 2005, A forms *DST*, a Delaware statutory trust described in the Delaware Statutory Trust Act, Del. Code Ann. title 12, §§ 3801 - 3824, to hold property for investment. A contributes Blackacre to *DST*. Upon contribution, *DST* assumes A's rights and obligations under the note with *BK* and the lease with Z. In accordance with the terms of the note, neither *DST* nor any of its beneficial owners are personally liable to *BK* on the note, which continues to be secured by Blackacre.

The trust agreement provides that interests in *DST* are freely transferable. However, *DST* interests are not publicly traded on an established securities market. *DST* will terminate on the earlier of 10 years from the date of its creation or the disposition of Blackacre, but will not terminate on the bankruptcy, death, or incapacity of any owner or on the transfer of any right, title, or interest of the owners. The trust agreement further provides that interests in *DST* will be of a single class, representing undivided beneficial interests in the assets of *DST*.

Under the trust agreement, the trustee is authorized to establish a reasonable reserve for expenses associated with holding Blackacre that may be payable out of trust funds. The trustee is required to distribute all available cash less reserves quarterly to each beneficial owner in proportion to their respective interests in *DST*. The trustee is required to invest cash received from Blackacre between each quarterly distribution and all cash held in reserve in short-term obligations of (or guaranteed by) the United States, or any agency or instrumentality thereof, and in certificates of deposit of any bank or trust company having a minimum stated surplus and capital. The trustee is permitted to invest only in obligations maturing prior to the next distribution date and is required to hold such obligations until maturity. In addition to the right to a quarterly distribution of cash, each beneficial owner has the right to an in-kind distribution of its proportionate share of trust property.

The trust agreement provides that the trustee's activities are limited to the collection and distribution of income. The trustee may not exchange Blackacre for other property, purchase assets other than the short-term investments described above, or accept additional contributions of assets (including money) to *DST*. The trustee may not renegotiate the terms of the debt used to acquire Blackacre and may not renegotiate the lease with Z or enter into leases with tenants other than Z, except in the case of Z's bankruptcy or insolvency. In addition, the trustee may make only minor non-structural modifications to Blackacre, unless otherwise required by law. The trust agreement further provides that the trustee may engage in ministerial activities to the extent required to maintain and operate *DST* under local law.

On January 3, 2005, *B* and *C* exchange Whiteacre and Greenacre, respectively, for all of *A*'s interests in *DST* through a qualified intermediary, within the meaning of § 1.1031(k)-1(g). *A* does not engage in a § 1031 exchange. Whiteacre and Greenacre were held for investment and are of like kind to Blackacre, within the meaning of § 1031.

Neither *DST* nor its trustee enters into a written agreement with *A*, *B*, or *C*, creating an agency relationship. In dealings with third parties, neither *DST* nor its trustee is represented as an agent of *A*, *B*, or *C*.

BK is not related to *A*, *B*, *C*, *DST*'s trustee or *Z* within the meaning of § 267(b) or § 707(b). *Z* is not related to *B*, *C*, or *DST*'s trustee within the meaning of § 267(b) or § 707(b).

LAW

Delaware law provides that a Delaware statutory trust is an unincorporated association recognized as an entity separate from its owners. A Delaware statutory trust is created by executing a governing instrument and filing an executed certificate of trust. Creditors of the beneficial owners of a Delaware statutory trust may not assert claims directly against the property in the trust. A Delaware statutory trust may sue or be sued, and property held in a Delaware statutory trust is subject to attachment or execution as if the trust were a corporation. Beneficial owners of a Delaware statutory trust are entitled to the same limitation on personal liability because of actions of the Delaware statutory trust that is extended to stockholders of Delaware corporations. A Delaware statutory trust may merge or consolidate with or into one or more statutory entities or other business entities.

Section 671 provides that, where the grantor or another person is treated as the owner of any portion of a trust (commonly referred to as a "grantor trust"), there shall be included in computing the taxable income and credits of the grantor or the other person those items of income, deductions, and credits against tax of the trust which are attributable to that portion of the trust to the extent that the items would be taken into account under chapter 1 in computing taxable income or credits against the tax of an individual.

Section 1.671-2(e)(1) of the Income Tax Regulations provides that, for purposes of subchapter J, a grantor includes any person to the extent such person either creates a trust or directly or indirectly makes a gratuitous transfer of property to a trust.

Under § 1.671-2(e)(3), the term "grantor" includes any person who acquires an interest in a trust from a grantor of the trust if the interest acquired is an interest in certain investment trusts described in § 301.7701-4(c).

Under § 677(a), the grantor is treated as the owner of any portion of a trust whose income without the approval or consent of any adverse party is, or, in the discretion of the grantor or a nonadverse party, or both, may be distributed, or held or accumulated for future distribution, to the grantor or the grantor's spouse.

A person that is treated as the owner of an undivided fractional interest of a trust under subpart E of part I, subchapter J of the Code (§§ 671 and following), is considered to own the trust assets attributable to that undivided fractional interest of the trust for federal income tax purposes. *See* Rev. Rul. 88-103, 1988-2 C.B. 304; Rev. Rul. 85-45, 1985-1 C.B. 183; and Rev. Rul. 85-13, 1985-1 C.B. 184. *See also*§ 1.1001-2(c), *Example 5*.

Section 761(a) provides that the term "partnership" includes a syndicate, group, pool, joint venture, or other unincorporated organization through or by means of which any business, financial operation, or venture is carried on, and that is not a corporation or a trust or estate. Under regulations the Secretary may, at the election of all the members of the unincorporated organization, exclude such organization from the application of all or part of subchapter K, if the income of the members of the organization may be adequately determined without the computation of partnership taxable income and the organization is availed of (1) for investment purposes only and not for the active conduct of a business, (2) for the joint production, extraction, or use of property, but not for the purpose of selling services or property produced or extracted, or (3) by dealers in securities for a short period for the purpose of underwriting, selling, or distributing a particular issue of securities.

Section 1.761-2(a)(2) provides the requirements that must be satisfied for participants in the joint purchase, retention, sale, or exchange of investment property to elect to be excluded from the application of the provisions of subchapter K. One of these requirements is that the participants own the property as coowners.

Section 1031(a)(1) provides that no gain or loss is recognized on the exchange of property held for productive use in a trade or business or for investment if such property is exchanged solely for property of like kind that is to be held either for productive use in a trade or business or for investment.

Section 1031(a)(2) provides that § 1031(a) does not apply to any exchange of stocks, bonds or notes, other securities or evidences of indebtedness or interest, interests in a partnership, or certificates of trust or beneficial interests. It further provides that an interest in a partnership that has in effect a valid election under § 761(a) to be excluded from the application of all of subchapter K shall be treated as an interest in each of the assets of the partnership and not as an interest in a partnership.

Under § 301.7701-1(a)(1) of the Procedure and Administration Regulations, whether an organization is an entity separate from its owners for federal tax purposes is a matter of federal tax law and does not depend on whether the organization is recognized as an entity under local law.

Generally, when participants in a venture form a state law entity and avail themselves of the benefits of that entity for a valid business purpose, such as investment or profit, and not for tax avoidance, the entity will be recognized for federal tax purposes. *See Moline Properties, Inc. v. Comm'r*, 319 U.S. 436 (1943); *Zmuda v. Comm'r*, 731 F.2d 1417 (9th Cir. 1984); *Boca Investerings P'ship v. United States*, 314 F.3d 625 (D.C. Cir. 2003); *Saba P'ship v. Comm'r*, 273 F.3d 1135 (D.C. Cir. 2001); *ASA Investerings P'ship v. Comm'r*, 201 F.3d 505 (D.C. Cir. 2000); *Markosian v. Comm'r*, 73 T.C. 1235 (1980).

Section 301.7701-2(a) defines the term "business entity" as any entity recognized for federal tax purposes (including an entity with a single owner that may be disregarded as an entity separate from its owner under § 301.7701-3) that is not properly classified as a trust under § 301.7701-4 or otherwise subject to special treatment under the Code. A business entity with two or more owners is classified for federal tax purposes as either a corporation or a partnership. A business entity with only one owner is classified as a corporation or is disregarded.

Section 301.7701-3(a) provides that an eligible entity can elect its classification for federal tax purposes. Under § 301.7701-3(b)(1), unless the entity elects otherwise, a domestic eligible entity is a partnership if it has two or more owners or is disregarded as an entity separate from its owner if it has a single owner.

Section 301.7701-4(a) provides that the term "trust" refers to an arrangement created either by will or by an inter vivos declaration whereby trustees take title to property for the purpose of protecting and conserving it for the beneficiaries. Usually the beneficiaries of a trust do no more than accept the benefits thereof and are not voluntary planners or creators of the trust arrangement. However, the beneficiaries of a trust may be the persons who create it, and it will be recognized as a trust if it was created for the purpose of protecting and conserving the trust property for beneficiaries who stand in the same relation to the trust as they would if the trust had been created by others for them.

Section 301.7701-4(b) provides that there are other arrangements known as trusts because the legal title to property is conveyed to trustees for the benefit of beneficiaries, but that are not classified as trusts for federal tax purposes because they are not simply arrangements to protect or conserve the property for the beneficiaries. These trusts, which are often known as business or commercial trusts, generally are created by the beneficiaries simply as a device to carry on a profit-making business that normally would have been carried on through business organizations that are classified as corporations or partnerships.

Section 301.7701-4(c)(1) provides that an "investment" trust will not be classified as a trust if there is a power under the trust agreement to vary the investment of the certificate holders. *See Comm'r v. North American Bond Trust*, 122 F.2d 545 (2d Cir. 1941), *cert. denied*, 314 U.S. 701 (1942). An investment trust with a single class of ownership interests, representing undivided beneficial interests in the assets of the trust, will be classified as a trust if there is no power to vary the investment of the certificate holders.

A power to vary the investment of the certificate holders exists where there is a managerial power, under the trust instrument, that enables a trust to take advantage of variations in the market to improve the investment of the investors. *See Comm'r v. North American Bond Trust*, 122 F.2d at 546.

Rev. Rul. 75-192, 1975-1 C.B. 384, discusses the situation where a provision in the trust agreement requires the trustee to invest cash on hand between the quarterly distribution dates. The trustee is required to invest the money in short-term obligations of (or guaranteed by) the United States, or any agency or instrumentality thereof, and in certificates of deposit of any bank or trust company having a minimum stated surplus and capital. The trustee is permitted to invest only in obligations maturing prior to the next distribution date and is required to hold such obligations until maturity. Rev. Rul. 75-192 concludes that, because the restrictions on the types of permitted investments limit the trustee to a fixed return similar to that earned on a bank account and eliminate any opportunity to profit from market fluctuations, the power to invest in the specified kinds of short-term investments is not a power to vary the trust's investment.

Rev. Rul. 78-371, 1978-2 C.B. 344, concludes that a trust established by the heirs of a number of contiguous parcels of real estate is an association taxable as a corporation for federal tax purposes where the trustees have the power to purchase and sell contiguous or adjacent real estate, accept or retain contributions of contiguous or adjacent real estate, raze or erect any building or structure, make any improvements to the land originally contributed, borrow money, and mortgage or lease the property. *Compare* Rev. Rul. 79-77, 1979-1 C.B. 448 (concluding that a trust formed by three parties to hold a single parcel of real estate is classified as a trust for federal income tax purposes when the trustee has limited powers that do not evidence an intent to carry on a profit making business).

Rev. Rul. 92-105, 1992-2 C.B. 204, addresses the transfer of a taxpayer's interest in an Illinois land trust under § 1031. Under the facts of the ruling, a single taxpayer created an Illinois land trust and named a domestic corporation as trustee. Under the deed of trust, the taxpayer transferred legal and equitable title to real property to the trust, subject to the provisions of an accompanying land trust agreement. The land trust agreement provided that the taxpayer retained exclusive control of the management, operation, renting, and selling of the real property, together with an exclusive right to the earnings and proceeds from the real property. Under the agreement, the taxpayer was required to file all tax returns, pay all taxes, and satisfy any other liabilities with respect to the real property. Rev. Rul 92-105 concludes that, because the trustee's only responsibility was to hold and transfer title at the direction of the taxpayer, a trust, as defined in § 301.7701-4(a), was not established. Moreover, there were no other arrangements between the taxpayer and the trustee (or between the taxpayer and any other person) that would cause the overall arrangement to be classified as a partnership (or any other type of entity). Instead, the trustee was a mere agent for the holding and transfer of title to real property, and the taxpayer retained direct ownership of the real property for federal income tax purposes.

ANALYSIS

Under Delaware law, *DST* is an entity that is recognized as separate from its owners. Creditors of the beneficial owners of *DST* may not assert claims directly against Blackacre. *DST* may sue or be sued, and the property of *DST* is subject to attachment and execution as if it were a corporation. The beneficial owners of *DST* are entitled to the same limitation on personal liability because of actions of *DST* that is extended to stockholders of Delaware corporations. *DST* may merge or consolidate with or into one or more statutory entities or other business entities. *DST* is formed for investment purposes. Thus, *DST* is an entity for federal tax purposes.

Whether *DST* or its trustee is an agent of *DST*'s beneficial owners depends upon the arrangement between the parties. The beneficiaries of *DST* do not enter into an agency agreement with *DST* or its trustee. Further, neither *DST* nor its trustee acts as an agent for *A*, *B*, or *C* in dealings with third parties. Thus, neither *DST* nor its trustee is the agent of *DST*'s beneficial owners. *Cf. Comm'r v. Bollinger*, 485 U.S. 340 (1988).

This situation is distinguishable from Rev. Rul. 92-105. First, in Rev. Rul. 92-105, the beneficiary retained the direct obligation to pay liabilities and taxes relating to the property. *DST*, in contrast, assumed *A*'s obligations on the lease with *Z* and on the loan with *BK*, and Delaware law provides the beneficial owners of *DST* with the same limitation on personal liability extended to shareholders of Delaware corporations. Second, unlike *A*, the beneficiary in Rev. Rul. 92-105 retained the right to manage and control the trust property.

Issue 1. Classification of Delaware Statutory Trust

Because *DST* is an entity separate from its owner, *DST* is either a trust or a business entity for federal tax purposes. To determine whether *DST* is a trust or a business entity for federal tax purposes, it is necessary, under § 301.7701-4(c)(1), to determine whether there is a power under the trust agreement to vary the investment of the certificate holders.

Prior to, but on the same date as, the transfer of Blackacre to *DST*, *A* entered into a 10-year nonrecourse loan secured by Blackacre. *A* also entered into the 10-year net lease agreement with *Z*. *A*'s rights and obligations under the loan and lease were assumed by *DST*. Because the duration of *DST* is 10 years (unless Blackacre is disposed of prior to that time), the financing and leasing arrangements related to Blackacre that were made prior to the inception of *DST* are fixed for the entire life of *DST*. Further, the trustee may only invest in short-term obligations that mature prior to the next distribution date and is required to hold these obligations until maturity. Because the trust agreement requires that any cash from Blackacre, and any cash earned on short-term obligations held by *DST* between distribution dates, be distributed quarterly, and because the disposition of Blackacre results in the termination of *DST*, no reinvestment of such monies is possible.

The trust agreement provides that the trustee's activities are limited to the collection and distribution of income. The trustee may not exchange Blackacre for other property, purchase assets other than the short-term investments described above, or accept additional contributions of assets (including money) to *DST*. The trustee may not renegotiate the terms of the debt used to acquire Blackacre and may not renegotiate the lease with *Z* or enter into leases with tenants other than *Z*, except in the case of *Z*'s bankruptcy or insolvency. In addition, the trustee may make only minor non-structural modifications to Blackacre, unless otherwise required by law.

This situation is distinguishable from Rev. Rul. 78-371, because *DST*'s trustee has none of the powers described in Rev. Rul. 78-371, which evidence an intent to carry on a profit making business. Because all of the interests in *DST* are of a single class representing undivided beneficial interests in the assets of *DST* and *DST*'s trustee has no power to vary the investment of the certificate holders to benefit from variations in the market, *DST* is an investment trust that will be classified as a trust under § 301.7701-4(c)(1).

Issue 2. Exchange of Real Property for Interests under § 1031

B and *C* are treated as grantors of the trust under § 1.671-2(e)(3) when they acquire their interests in the trust from *A*. Because they have the right to distributions of all trust income attributable to their undivided fractional interests in the trust, *B* and *C* are each treated, by reason of § 677, as the owner of an *aliquot* portion of the trust and all income, deductions, and credits attributable to that portion are includible by *B* and *C* under § 671 in computing their taxable income. Because the owner of an undivided fractional interest of a trust is considered to own the trust assets attributable to that interest for federal income tax purposes, *B* and *C* are each considered to own an undivided fractional interest in Blackacre for federal income tax purposes. See Rev. Rul. 85-13.

Accordingly, the exchange of real property by *B* and *C* for an interest in *DST* through a qualified intermediary is the exchange of real property for an interest in Blackacre, and not the exchange of real property for a certificate of trust or beneficial interest under § 1031(a)(2)(E). Because Whiteacre and Greenacre are of like kind to Blackacre, and provided the other requirements of § 1031 are satisfied, the exchange of real property for an interest in *DST* by *B* and *C* will qualify for nonrecognition of gain or loss under § 1031. Moreover, because *DST* is a grantor trust, the outcome to the parties will remain the same, even if *A* transfers interests in Blackacre directly to *B* and *C*, and *B* and *C* immediately form *DST* by contributing their interests in Blackacre.

Under the facts of this case, if *DST*'s trustee has additional powers under the trust agreement such as the power to do one or more of the following: (i) dispose of Blackacre and acquire new property; (ii) renegotiate the lease with *Z* or enter into leases with tenants other than *Z*; (iii) renegotiate or refinance the obligation used to purchase Blackacre; (iv) invest cash received to profit from market fluctuations; or (v) make more than minor non-structural modifications to Blackacre not required by law, *DST* will be a business entity which, if it has two or more owners, will be classified as a partnership for federal tax purposes, unless it is treated as a corporation under § 7704 or elects to be classified as a corporation under § 301.7701-3. In addition, because the assets of *DST* will not be owned by the beneficiaries as co-owners under state law, *DST* will not be able to elect to be excluded from the application of subchapter K. *See* § 1.761-2(a)(2)(i).

HOLDINGS

(1) The Delaware statutory trust described above is an investment trust, under § 301.7701-4(c), that will be classified as a trust for federal tax purposes.

(2) A taxpayer may exchange real property for an interest in the Delaware statutory trust described above without recognition of gain or loss under § 1031, if the other requirements of § 1031 are satisfied.

EFFECT ON OTHER REVENUE RULINGS

Rev. Rul. 78-371 and Rev. Rul. 92-105 are distinguished.

DRAFTING INFORMATION

The principal author of this revenue ruling is Christopher L. Trump of the Office of Associate Chief Counsel (Pass-throughs and Special Industries). For further information regarding this revenue ruling, contact Christopher L. Trump at (202) 622-3070 (not a toll-free call).

APPENDIX

LIKE-KIND COALITION LETTER TO SENATE FINANCE COMMITTEE

May 10, 2016

The Honorable Orrin G. Hatch
Chairman
Senate Committee on Finance
219 Dirksen Senate Office Building
Washington, D.C. 20510

The Honorable Ronald L. Wyden
Ranking Member
Senate Committee on Finance
219 Dirksen Senate Office Building
Washington, D.C. 20510

Dear Chairman Hatch and Ranking Member Wyden:

As the Senate Finance Committee considers ways to create jobs, grow the economy, and raise wages, we strongly urge you to retain current law regarding like-kind exchanges under section 1031 of the Internal Revenue Code ("Code"). Like-kind exchanges are integral to the efficient operation and ongoing vitality of thousands of American businesses, which in turn strengthen the U.S. economy and create jobs. Like-kind exchanges allow taxpayers to exchange their property for more productive like-kind property, to diversify or consolidate holdings, and to transition to meet changing business needs. Specifically, section 1031 provides that firms and investors do not immediately recognize a gain or loss when they exchange assets for "like-kind" property that will be used in their trade or business. They do immediately recognize gain, however, to the extent that cash or other "boot" is received. Importantly, like-kind exchanges are similar to other non-recognition and tax deferral provisions in the Code because they result in no change to the economic position of the taxpayer.

Since 1921, like-kind exchanges have encouraged capital investment in the United States by allowing funds to be reinvested in the enterprise, which is the very reason section 1031 was enacted in the first place. These investments not only benefit the companies making the like-kind exchanges, but also suppliers, manufacturers, and others facilitating them. Like-kind exchanges ensure both the best use of real estate and a new and used personal property market that significantly benefits start-ups and small businesses. Eliminating them or restricting their use would have a contraction effect on our economy by increasing the cost of capital. In fact, a recent macroeconomic analysis by Ernst & Young found that limitations on like-kind exchanges could lead to a decline in U.S. GDP of up to $13.1 billion annually.[1]

---

[1] *Economic Impact of Repealing Like-Kind Exchange Rules*, Ernst & Young (March 2015, revised November 2015), at (iii), *available at* http://www.1031taxreform.com/wp-content/uploads/EY-Report-for-LKE-Coalition-onmacroeconomic-impact-of-repealing-LKE-rules-revised-2015-11-18.pdf.

Companies in a wide range of industries, business structures, and sizes rely on the likekind exchange provision of the Code. These businesses—which include construction, industrial, and farm equipment; vehicle manufacturers and lessors; and real estate—provide essential products and services to U.S. consumers and are an integral part of our economy. A study by researchers at the University of Florida and Syracuse University supports that without like-kind exchanges, businesses and entrepreneurs would have less incentive and ability to make real estate and capital investments. The immediate recognition of a gain upon the disposition of property being replaced would impair cash flow and could make it uneconomical to replace that asset.[2] As a result, requiring the recognition of gain on like-kind exchanges would hamper the ability of businesses to be competitive in our global marketplace. The reduced investment in real estate and capital would also have significant upstream and downstream impacts on economic reactivity and employment in industries as diverse as real estate, agriculture, construction, tourism, hospitality, trucking, and equipment supply.

In summary, there is strong economic rationale, supported by recent analytical research, for the like-kind exchange provision's nearly 100-year existence in the Code. Limitation or repeal of section 1031 would deter and, in many cases, prohibit continued and new real estate and capital investment. These adverse effects on the U.S. economy would likely not be offset by lower tax rates. Finally, like-kind exchanges promote uniformly agreed upon tax reform goals such as economic growth, job creation and increased competitiveness.

Thank you for your consideration of this important matter.

Sincerely,

American Car Rental AssociationAmerican Farm Bureau Federation
American Truck Dealers
American Trucking Associations
Asian American Hotel Owners Association
Associated General Contractors of America
Avis Budget Group, Inc.
CCIM Institute

---

[2] David Ling and Milena Petrova, *The Economic Impact of Repealing or Limiting Section 1031 Like-Kind Exchanges in Real Estate* (March 215, revised June 2015), at 5, *available at* http://www.1031taxreform.com/wpcontent/ uploads/Ling-Petrova-Economic-Impact-of-Repealing-or-Limiting-Section-1031-in-Real-Estate.pdf.

C.R. England, Inc.
Equipment Leasing and Finance Association
Federation of Exchange Accommodators
Hertz Global Holdings, Inc.
Idaho Dairymen's Association
Institute of Real Estate Management
National Apartment Association
National Association of Real Estate Investment Trusts
National Association of Realtors ®
National Automobile Dealers Association
National Multifamily Housing Council
National Stone, Sand, and Gravel Association
National Utility Contractors Association
The Real Estate Roundtable
Realtors ® Land Institute
South East Dairy Farmers Association
Truck Renting and Leasing Association
Western United Dairymen

1031 GLOSSARY

1031 Exchange

The sale or disposition of real estate or personal property (relinquished property) held for productive use in a trade or business or for investment and the acquisition of like-kind real estate or personal property (replacement property) structured as a tax-deferred, like-kind exchange transaction pursuant to Section 1031 of the Internal Revenue Code to defer federal and state taxes, capital gains, and depreciation recapture taxes.

Accelerated Depreciation

A depreciation method that allows you to deduct a greater portion of the cost of depreciable property in the first years after the property is placed in service, rather than spreading the cost evenly over the life of the asset, as with the straight-line depreciation method.

Accommodator

An unrelated party who participates in the tax-deferred, like-kind exchange to facilitate the disposition of the Exchanger's relinquished property and the acquisition of the Exchanger's replacement property. The Accommodator has no economic interest except for any compensation (exchange fee) it may receive for acting as an Accommodator in facilitating the exchange as defined in Section 1031 of the Internal

Revenue Code. The Accommodator is technically referred to as the Qualified Intermediary, but is also known as the Accommodator, Facilitator, or Intermediary.

Actual Possession/Receipt

Direct access to your exchange funds or other property. Receiving exchange funds during the exchange period will disqualify your exchange. Also called Constructive Receipt.

Adjusted Basis

The Original Basis plus any improvement costs minus the full depreciation on the property. Adjusted Basis is used to determine the amount of capital gain that you derive from a sale. It is also used to determine the amount that can be depreciated on a replacement property. To determine the adjusted cost basis for your property, you must start with the original purchase cost. You then add your purchasing expenses, your cost of capital improvements, and principal payments of special assessments (sewer and streets) to the property, and then subtract depreciation you have taken or were allowed to take, any casualty losses taken, and any demolition losses taken.

Agent

An entity that acts on behalf of a principal, e.g., the taxpayer. A Qualified Intermediary cannot be your agent at the time of or during a tax-deferred, like-kind exchange. For 1031 Exchange purposes, an agent includes any employee, attorney, accountant or investment banker, or real estate agent or broker within the two-year period prior to the transfer of your first relinquished property. An agency relationship does not exist with entities that offer Section 1031 Exchanges services or routine title, escrow, trust, or financial services.

Agreement for Transfer

Purchase agreement, offer and acceptance, sale agreement, earnest money agreement, real estate contract, or other contract contemplating the purchase or sale of real property.

Asset Class

A category of investments that contain similar characteristics, e.g., retail, residential, commercial office, medical, senior housing, etc.

Balancing the Exchange

A balanced exchange ensures that the taxpayer defers 100% of his or her taxes on capital gain and depreciation recapture. To achieve a balanced exchange: 1) acquire a replacement property that is equal to or greater than the relinquished property; 2) reinvest all the net equity from the relinquished property in the replacement property; and 3) assume debt on the replacement property that is equal to or greater than the debt on the replacement property or contribute cash to make up the deficiency.

Basis

The original purchase price or cost of your property plus any out-of-pocket expenses, such as brokerage commissions, escrow costs, title insurance premiums, sales tax (if personal property), and other closing costs directly related to the acquisition. See also *Original Basis* and *Net-Adjusted Basis*.

Boot

This is the property the taxpayer receives in the exchange that does not qualify as like-kind property. Cash proceeds are the most common form of boot and a boot is subject to taxation. Boot is taxable to the extent there is a capital gain.

Build-to-Suit Exchange

A tax-deferred, like-kind exchange whereby the Qualified Intermediary or Exchange Accommodation Titleholder acquires and holds the title to the replacement property on behalf of the Exchanger, during which time structures or improvements are constructed or installed on or within the replacement property. Also known as an Improvement Exchange.

Business Assets

Real property, tangible depreciable property, intangible property, and other types of property contained or used in a business. Exchanging one business for another business is not permitted under Internal Revenue Code Section 1031. However, taxpayers may exchange business assets on an asset-by-asset basis, usually as part of a Mixed-Property (Multi-Asset) Exchange.

Capital Gain

The capital gain is calculated as follows: total selling price of the relinquished property, less exchange expenses, less the relinquished property's adjusted basis. The adjusted basis is the original cost, plus the cost of capital improvements, less depreciation or cost recovery deductions. Capital gains may be subject to depreciation recapture and other IRS rules.

Capital Gains Tax

Tax levied by federal and state governments on investments that are held for one year or more. Investments may include real estate, stocks, bonds, collectibles, and tangible depreciable personal property. Capital gain taxes currently range from 15% to 20%, depending on tax bracket.

Capital Improvements

For land or buildings, improvements (also known as capital improvements) are the expenses of permanently upgrading your property rather than maintaining or repairing it. Instead of taking a deduction for the cost of improvements in the year paid, you add the cost of the improvements to the basis of the property. If the property you improved is a building that is being depreciated, you must depreciate the improvements over the same useful life as the building.

Capitalization Rate (Cap Rate)

The rate of return an investor wants to achieve on real property. The capitalization rate can provide for both the return **of** the investment and the return **on** the investment (profit). To obtain a property's capitalization rate, divide the net operating income of a property by its value. To determine a property's value, divide the property's net operating income by the desired capitalization rate. In the Income Capitalization Method of real property appraisal, a capitalization rate is used to appraise a property's value. The Income Capitalization Method of appraisal is used to value investment property, such as apartment buildings, commercial office buildings, and retail malls.

Cash Equivalents

Short-term investments, such as U.S. Treasury securities, certificates of deposit, and money market fund shares, that can easily be liquidated into cash. Exchange funds held by an Accommodator may be invested in income-producing cash equivalents prior to funds being utilized to conclude a purchase of a replacement property.

Concurrent Exchange

A tax-deferred, like-kind exchange transaction whereby the disposition of the relinquished property and the acquisition of the replacement property close or transfer at the same time. Also referred to as a Simultaneous Exchange.

Construction 1031 Exchange

An exchange involving a replacement property that is not yet built. Improvements on the property are completed prior to the expiration of the 180 days. In a Construction 1031 Exchange, the property is held by a specially formed limited liability company called the Exchange Accommodation Taxpayer. A Construction Exchange generally has greater complexity and higher fees than a 1031 Exchange.

Constructive Receipt

Exercising control over your exchange funds or other property. Control over your exchange funds includes having money or property from the exchange credited to your bank account or property or funds reserved for you. Being in constructive receipt of exchange funds or property may result in the disallowance of the tax-deferred, like-kind exchange transaction, thereby creating a taxable sale.

Contract 1031 Exchange

A Contract Exchange is the tax-deferred exchange of the Buyer's ownership in a Sales Contract on real property, for different real property, or for a contract or option on different real property; or the Option Holder's exchange of an Option to purchase real property, for different real property, or for an option or contract on different real property. Essentially, a Contract Exchange is a 1031 exchange of an open option to purchase, or an open Sales Contract, rather than a 1031 exchange of the underlying real estate itself.

Cooperation Clause

Language to be included in the Purchase and Sale Contracts for both relinquished and replacement property that indicates and discloses that the transaction is part of an intended tax-deferred, like-kind exchange transaction and requires that all parties cooperate in completing said exchange.

Delaware Statutory Trust (DST)

A Delaware Statutory Trust (DST) is a separate legal entity created as a trust under the laws of Delaware in which each owner has a beneficial interest in the DST for federal income tax purposes and is treated as owning an undivided fractional interest in the property. In 2004, the IRS released Revenue Ruling 2004-86, which allows the use of a DST to acquire real estate where the beneficial interests in the trust will be treated as direct interests in replacement property for purposes of conducting 1031 exchanges.

Depreciation

A reduction in value of a property over the property's economic life. The IRS requires investors and business owners to take a tax deduction on the amount of a property's depreciation. The practice of amortizing or spreading the cost of depreciable property over a specified period, usually its estimated depreciable life. To put it another way, you are allowed a deduction on your income tax return for the wearing away and expensing over time of property or assets, such as aircraft, vehicles, livestock, and buildings. A depreciable asset is a capital expenditure in depreciable property used in a trade or business or held to produce income and has a definite useful life of more than one year. Non-depreciable property includes vacant land. For assets that have an expected useful life of more than one year, you spread the cost of the asset over its estimated useful life rather than deducting the entire cost in the year you place the asset in service. The tax code (law) specifies the depreciation period for specific types of assets.

Depreciation Recapture

The amount of gain resulting from the disposition of property that represents the recovery of depreciation expense that has been previously deducted on the Taxpayer's (Exchanger's) income tax returns.

Direct Deeding

A practice authorized by Treasury Revenue Ruling 90-34 whereby either the relinquished property or the replacement property can be deeded directly from seller to buyer without deeding the property to the Qualified Intermediary.

Disposition

The sale or other disposal of property that causes a gain or a loss, including like-kind exchanges and involuntary conversions.

Disqualified Person

Typically an agent of the taxpayer at the time of the transaction. An agent includes any person who has acted as the taxpayer's employee, attorney, accountant, investment banker or broker, or real estate agent, or broker within two years of the taxpayer's transfer of relinquished property. Services such as routine financial, title insurance, escrow, or trust services provided to the taxpayer by a financial institution, title insurance company, or escrow company are not considered.

Exchange Accommodation Taxpayer (EAT)

The Exchange Accommodation Taxpayer (EAT) is a specially formed limited liability company used during a Construction Exchange or a Reverse Exchange. An EAT is an unrelated party that customarily holds the title of either the replacement or relinquished property to facilitate a reverse or build-to-suit tax-deferred, like-kind exchange transaction.

Exchange Agreement

The written agreement defining the transfer of the relinquished property, the subsequent receipt of the replacement property, and the restrictions on the exchange proceeds during the exchange period. The Exchange Agreement is typically provided by the Accommodator.

Exchange Period

A 180-day window in which the Exchanger must complete a tax-deferred exchange. During the exchange period, there is a 45-day identification period in which the Exchanger must identify which property or properties will be purchased. If the 180th day falls after the due date of the Exchanger's tax return, an extension may be filed to receive the full 180-day exchange period.

Exchanger

The actual owner of the investment property looking to make a tax-deferred exchange.

Exchange Funds Account

The account established by the Qualified Intermediary (QI) to hold the exchange funds.

Excluded Property

The rules for like-kind exchanges do not apply to property held for personal use (such as homes, boats, or cars); cash; stock in trade or other property held primarily for sale (such as inventories, raw materials, and real estate held by dealers); stocks, bonds, notes, or other securities or evidences of indebtedness (such as accounts receivable); partnership interests; certificates of trust or beneficial interest; chooses in action.

The Fair Market Value

This is the likely selling price as defined by the market at a specific point in time.

Forward Delayed Exchange

A type of exchange that occurs when a property is sold (relinquished property) and another property is purchased (replacement property) within 180 days following the sale of the relinquished property.

Gross Multiplier

A variation on the Income Capitalization Method of appraising property. The Gross Multiplier approach is a way to obtain a fast, rough estimate of a property's value. In this approach, a monthly or annual number is multiplied by a property's gross income to obtain the property's value. Dividing the sale price of a similar property by its gross income provides its gross multiplier.

Identification

A written, unambiguous description of the intended replacement property or properties, signed by the Exchanger must be sent to the Qualified Intermediary or other person who is a party to the exchange and who is not a disqualified person.

Identification Period

The time that begins upon the close of escrow of the relinquished property. During this 45-day period, the 1031 Exchanger must identify the replacement property to continue with the Section 1031 exchange transaction. The identification period is the initial 45 days of the overall 180-day window, during which the replacement property or properties need to be acquired to complete the exchange.

Identification Removal

An Identification Removal form is used to remove previously identified replacement property or properties within the identification period of 45 days.

Identification Statement

An Identification Statement form is used to identify potential Replacement Property or Properties.

Improvement Exchange

A tax-deferred, like-kind exchange whereby the Qualified Intermediary or Exchange Accommodation Titleholder acquires and holds the title to the replacement property on behalf of Exchanger, during which time new or additional structures or improvements are constructed or installed on or within the replacement property. Also known as a Build-To-Suit Exchange.

Improvements

For land or buildings, improvements (also known as capital improvements) are the expenses of permanently upgrading your property rather than maintaining or repairing it. Instead of taking a deduction for the cost of improvements in the year paid, you add the cost of the improvements to the basis of the property. If the property you improved is a building that is being depreciated, you must depreciate the improvements over the same useful life as the building.

Intermediary

An unrelated party who participates in the tax-deferred, like-kind exchange to facilitate the disposition of the Exchanger's relinquished property and the acquisition of the Exchanger's replacement property. The Intermediary has no economic interest except for any compensation (exchange fee) it may receive for acting as an Intermediary in facilitating the exchange as defined in Section 1031 of the Internal Revenue Code. The Intermediary is technically referred to as the Qualified Intermediary, but is also known as the Accommodator, Facilitator, or Intermediary.

IRC 1031 Tax Code

Internal Revenue Code Section 1031.

Like-Class and Like-Kind Personal Property

Refers to the nature or character of the property and not to its grade or quality. Personal property listed or contained within the same general asset classification or product classification (SIC Code) will be of like-class and therefore like-kind.

Like-Kind Property

The properties involved in a tax-deferred exchange must be similar in nature or characteristics. *Like-kind* real estate property is effectively any real estate that is *not* your personal residence or *not* a second home.

Mixed Property (Multi-Asset) Exchange

An exchange that contains different types of properties such as depreciable tangible personal property, real property, and intangible personal property. In a Mixed Property Exchange, relinquished properties are segmented in like-kind groups and matched with corresponding like-kind groups of replacement properties.

Modified Accelerated Cost Recover Systems (MACRS)

The depreciation method generally used since 1986 for writing off the value of depreciable property, other than real estate, over time. MACRS allows you to write off the cost of assets faster than the straight-line depreciation method.

Mortgage Boot

This occurs when the Exchanger does not acquire debt that is equal to or greater than the debt that was paid off on the relinquished property sale; also referred to as debt relief. This creates a taxable event.

Napkin Test

A simple exercise to determine the potential for exposing taxable assets or boot in an exchange. The Napkin Test compares the value, equity, and mortgage of the relinquished and replacement properties. By going across or up in value, equity, and mortgage, there is no taxable boot in the exchange. The calculations are based on the following: if, when subtracting the relinquished property value from the replacement property value, a zero or positive amount is given, then there is no taxable boot. If a negative amount is given, then taxes are paid on that amount.

Net-Adjusted Basis

Used to determine the amount of capital gain that you derive from a sale. It is also used to determine the amount that can be depreciated on a replacement property. Net-Adjusted basis is calculated by taking the original purchase price, adding all capital improvements, and then subtracting total depreciation taken during your ownership period.

Net Operating Income

A property's gross income (scheduled rents and 100% vacancy factor) less its total annual expenses (including management costs, utilities, services, repairs, a vacancy factor, and a credit loss factor) plus any other additional income (vending machines, coin laundry operations, etc.).

Principal and interest payments on the mortgage and tax liability are not included.

Original Basis

Your original purchase price. The amount that you originally paid for your property is split between land value and building value. Building value can be depreciated, whereas land cannot be. Residential properties can be depreciated over 27.5 years, and non-residential properties can be depreciated over thirty-nine years.

Parking Arrangement

A process or procedure whereby either the Exchanger's relinquished property or replacement property is acquired by an Exchange Accommodation Titleholder (EAT) to facilitate a reverse or build-to-suit tax-deferred, like-kind exchange transaction pursuant to Treasury Revenue Ruling 2000-37.

Partial Exchange

An exchange that entails receiving cash, excluded property or non-like-kind property or any net reduction in debt (mortgage relief) on the replacement property, as well as an exchange of qualified, like-kind property. In the case of a partial exchange, tax liability would be incurred on the non-qualifying portion and capital gain deferred on the qualifying portion under Internal Revenue Code Section 1031.

Partial Tax Deferment

A tax that is owed by the taxpayer, of which part of the tax is paid to the IRS when taxes are due. The remaining tax is postponed to a time when a new taxable event occurs.

Principal Residence Exemption

Exclusion from capital gains tax on the sale of principal residence of $250,000 for individual taxpayers and $500,000 for couples, filing jointly, under Internal Revenue Code Section 121. Property must have been the principal residence of the taxpayer(s) twenty-four months out of the last sixty months. In the case of a dual-use property, such as a ranch, retail store, duplex, or triplex, the taxpayer can defer taxes on the portion of the property used for business or investment under Internal Revenue Code Section 1031 and exclude capital gain on the portion used as the primary residence under Section 121.

Personal Property

Any property belonging to the 1031 exchanger that is non-real estate-related.

Phase 1

The process in which the relinquished property is sold and all the respective paperwork for that process is completed. This process is also known as the down leg of the tax-deferred exchange process.

Phase 2

This is the process in which the replacement property is bought and all the respective paperwork for that process is completed. This process is also known as the up leg of the tax-deferred exchange process.

Qualified Escrow Account

An escrow account, wherein the Escrow Agent is not the Exchanger or a disqualified person and that limits the Exchanger's rights to receive, pledge, borrow, or otherwise obtain the benefits of the tax-deferred, like-kind exchange cash balance or other assets from the sale of the relinquished property in compliance with Treasury regulations. The Qualified Escrow Account also ensures that the Exchanger's exchange funds or assets are held as fiduciary funds and are therefore protected against claims from potential creditors of the Qualified Intermediary.

Qualified Intermediary

The Intermediary is also known as a QI, Accommodator, Facilitator, or Qualified Escrow Holder. A third party that helps to facilitate the exchange. The Qualified Intermediary has no economic interest except for any compensation (exchange fee) it may receive for facilitating the exchange as defined in Section 1031 of the Internal Revenue Code.

Qualified Trust Account

A trust, wherein the trustee is not the Exchanger or a disqualified person and the Exchanger's rights to receive, pledge, borrow, or otherwise obtain the benefits of the tax-deferred, like-kind exchange cash balance or other assets from the sale of the relinquished property in compliance with the Treasury regulations are limited. The qualified trust account also ensures that the Exchanger's exchange funds or assets are held as fiduciary funds and are therefore protected against claims from potential creditors of the Qualified Intermediary.

Qualified Use

An Exchanger must intend to use the property in their trade or business, to hold the property for investment, or to hold the property for income production to satisfy the qualified use test.

Real Estate Exchange

A type of Exchange of real property for real property. All types of real property are like-kind for other real property, including vacant land, residential, commercial, and even some long-term leases.

Real Property

Land and buildings (improvements), including but not limited to homes, apartment buildings, shopping centers, commercial buildings, factories, condominiums, leases of thirty years or more, quarries, and oil fields. All types of real property are exchangeable for all other types of real property. In general, state law determines what constitutes real property.

Relinquished Property

The original property being sold by the taxpayer when making a 1031 Exchange.

Replacement Property

The new property being acquired by the taxpayer when making a 1031 Exchange. Also referred to as the purchase, target, up leg, or Phase II property.

Reverse Exchanges

This is the type of exchange in which the replacement property is purchased before the sale of the relinquished property.

Rollover

A method by which an individual can transfer assets from one retirement program to another without the recognition of income for tax purposes. The requirements for a rollover depend on the type of program from which the distribution is made and the type of program receiving the distribution.

Rules of Identification

The guidelines that must be followed when making a tax-deferred 1031 Exchange, such as the Three-Property Rule, 200% Percent Rule, and 95% Percent Rule.

Safe Harbors

Treasury regulations provide certain safe harbors that assist Qualified Intermediaries and Exchangers in structuring tax-deferred, like-kind exchange transactions so they can be assured that no constructive receipt issues will be encountered during the exchange cycle.

Seller Carry-Back Financing

When the buyer of a property gives the seller of the property a note, secured by a deed of trust or mortgage. In a 1031 Exchange, seller carry-back financing is treated as boot, unless it is sold at a discount on the secondary market or assigned to the seller as a down payment on the replacement property.

Sequential Deeding

The former practice of transferring or deeding title to the Exchanger's relinquished property to the Qualified Intermediary first and then sequentially and immediately transferring or deeding title from the Qualified Intermediary to the buyer to properly structure a tax-deferred, like-kind exchange prior to the issuance of Treasury Revenue Ruling 90-34. Sequential deeding is used only in special tax-deferred, like-kind exchange transactions today that require special structuring (http://www.1031exchange.com/glossary).

Settlement Agent

Definitions include title agent, closing officer, escrow officer, settlement officer, closing agent, closing attorney, settlement attorney.

Simultaneous Exchange

A tax-deferred, like-kind exchange transaction whereby the disposition of the relinquished property and the acquisition of the replacement property close or transfer at the same time. Also referred to as a Concurrent Exchange.

Starker Exchange

Another common name for the tax-deferred, like-kind exchange transaction based on a court decision that was handed down in 1979 (*Starker v. Commissioner*). The Ninth Circuit Court of Appeals eventually agreed with Starker that its delayed tax-deferred, like-kind exchange transaction did in fact constitute a valid exchange pursuant to Section 1031 of the Internal Revenue Code. This ruling set the precedent for our current day delayed-exchange structures.

Straight-Line Depreciation Method

A depreciation method that spreads the cost or other basis of property evenly over its estimated useful life.

Tangible Personal Property

Property other than real estate that physically exists. Aircraft, business equipment, and vehicles are examples of tangible personal property. Assets such as trademarks, patents, and franchises only represent value and are therefore intangible property.

Tax Advisor

Financial advisor, accountant, CPA, tax attorney.

Taxpayer

Client, investor, or the exchanger.

Tax-Deferred Exchange

The procedure outlined under IRS Code Section 1031 involving a series of rules and regulations that must be met to take full advantage of deferring capital gains tax on the sale of investment real estate. Such 1031 tax-deferred exchanges are also commonly known as Starker exchanges, delayed exchanges, like-kind exchanges, 1031 exchanges, Section 1031 exchanges, tax-free exchanges, nontaxable exchanges, real estate exchanges, and real property exchanges. Although these terms refer to the same thing, the most typical term used today is the tax-deferred 1031 exchange.

Tenant in Common (TIC)

A fractional or partial ownership interest in a piece of property, rather than owning the entire piece of property. A TIC interest is made up of two or more individuals who have equal rights of possession. Co-tenants' interests may be equal or unequal and may be created at different times and using different conveyances. Each co-tenant has the right to dispose of or encumber his or her interest without the agreement of the other co-tenants. He or she cannot, however, encumber the entire property without the consent of all the co-tenants. In an Internal Revenue Code Section 1031 Exchange, an Exchanger may acquire a TIC interest with one or more other investors as his or her like-kind replacement property. For purposes of Internal Revenue Code Section 1031 Exchanges, a co-tenancy must only engage in investment activities, including supporting services that would typically accompany the investment. Co-tenants that are engaging in separate business activities are treated as partnerships by the IRS.

Titleholder

The entity that owns or holds title to property. In an Internal Revenue Code Section 1031 Exchange, the titleholder of the relinquished property must generally be the same as the titleholder of the replacement property. If a taxpayer dies prior to the acquisition of the replacement property, his or her estate may complete the exchange. When the acquisition and disposition entities bear the same taxpayer identification numbers, such as disregarded entities (single-member limited liability companies and revocable living trusts), the exchange usually qualifies.

Trust

A legal entity created by an individual in which one person or institution holds the right to manage property or assets for the benefit of someone else.

Trustee

An individual or institution appointed to administer a trust for its beneficiaries.

Three-Property Rule

The Exchanger may identify up to three properties, without regard to their value.

200% Percent Rule

The 1031 Exchanger may identify more than three properties, provided their combined fair market value does not exceed 200% of value of the relinquished property.

95% Percent Rule

The 1031 Exchanger may identify any number of properties, without regard to their value, provided the Exchanger acquires 95% of the fair market value of the properties identified.

INDEX

Symbols

A

B

C

D

E

F

I

L

M

N

O

P

Q

R

S

T